The Lake District

A Celebration of Cumbria

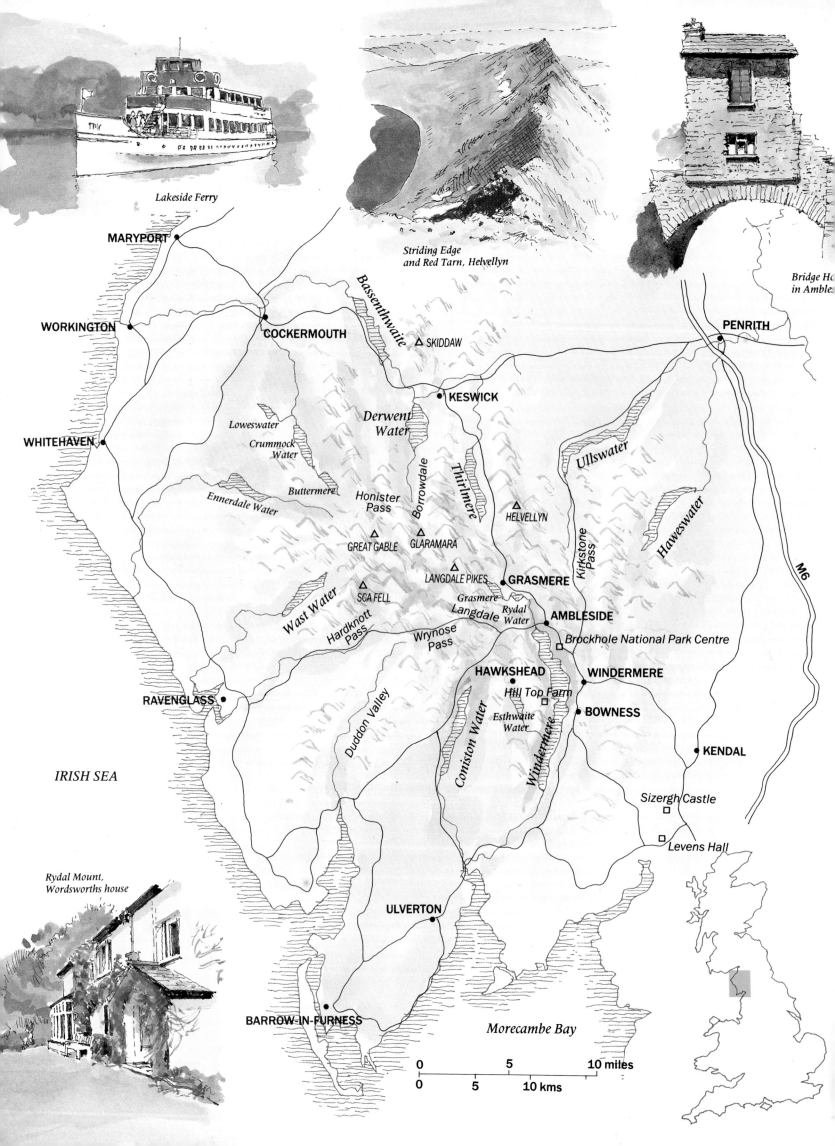

Lakeside Ferry

Striding Edge
and Red Tarn, Helvellyn

Bridge Ho
in Amble.

MARYPORT

WORKINGTON

COCKERMOUTH

Bassenthwaite

△ SKIDDAW

KESWICK

PENRITH

M6

WHITEHAVEN

Loweswater

Crummock
Water

Derwent
Water

Buttermere

Borrowdale

Thirlmere

Ullswater

Ennerdale Water

Honister
Pass

△ HELVELLYN

Haweswater

△ GREAT GABLE

△ GLARAMARA

Kirkstone
Pass

△ LANGDALE PIKES

Wast Water

△ SCA FELL

GRASMERE

Grasmere

AMBLESIDE

Langdale

Rydal
Water

Hardknott
Pass

Wrynose
Pass

Brockhole National Park Centre

HAWKSHEAD

WINDERMERE

Hill Top Farm

BOWNESS

Duddon Valley

Coniston Water

Esthwaite
Water

Windermere

KENDAL

IRISH SEA

Sizergh Castle

Levens Hall

Rydal Mount,
Wordsworths house

ULVERTON

BARROW-IN-FURNESS

Morecambe Bay

0   5   10 miles

0   5   10 kms

The Lake District

A Celebration of Cumbria

Edmund Swinglehurst

Photographs by Simon Warner

CAXTON EDITIONS

This Edition Published 2000 by
Caxton Editions an Imprint of
The Caxton Publishing Group

Produced by
Regency House Publishing Limited

Copyright © 1995 Regency House Publishing Limited

ISBN 1 84067 1165

All photographs supplied by Simon Warner, except
for pages 20, 22 bottom, 24 (both), 32 bottom, 48 left
and 76 top right, by Edmund Swinglehurst

Map supplied by Malcolm Porter

Printed in Hong Kong.

The publishers would like to thank The Trustees of
Rydal Mount for letting us photograph the interiors
of Rydal Mount and The Wordsworth Trust for
letting us photograph the interiors of Dove Cottage,
Grasmere.

Title page: Buttermere and the head of
               Crummock Water from Sourmilk Gill

These pages: Bannerdale from Martindale Church

Contents

Introduction

The English Lake District is a magically beautiful region of lakes and tarns, fells and high peaks just 40 miles across in Cumbria, in the north-west corner of England. It is visited by some twelve million hill walkers, climbers, holidaymakers and day trippers every year, yet remains miraculously unspoilt, a region of glorious vistas of reed-fringed stretches of water set in glacier-carved valleys dappled by sunlight, of breath-taking views from the highest peaks in England.

Lakes and mountains, as places where people could enjoy their leisure and commune with nature, began to enjoy popular favour in Europe from about the middle of the 18th century. For the 18th-century cultivated mind tutored by the new Romanticism, wild nature became the medium through which man could explore his spiritual being. New philosophical thought, spreading through Europe in reaction against the Age of Reason and a growing industrialisation, was encouraged by poets and writers who found in unspoiled nature the fulfilment of those romantic inclinations that the planned country house parks and cultivated farmlands of the age could not satisfy.

The field of action for this spiritual exercise was to be found preferably in uninhabited and picturesque places; the German poet, Goethe, found his inspiration in the gorges of the Rhine and the mountains of Switzerland which were also a spiritual kingdom for the English poets Shelley and Byron, both of whom also roamed further afield to Italy. In Britain, other poets found an Eden in the Lake District, a region which had been regarded for centuries as bleak and unwelcoming, suited only to rugged sheep farming.

The Lake District's most famous son is a poet, William Wordsworth, who was born in Cockermouth, in what was then the county of Cumberland, in 1770. Even at that time the general view of the region was changing. The poet Thomas Gray, best-known now for the wonderfully evocative 'Elegy in a Country Churchyard', had made two Lakeland tours

LEFT
The Langdale Pikes at dusk, silhouetted in the reed-fringed waters of Elter Water, the smallest of the Lake District's sixteen lakes. Several stretches of water designated 'tarns' are, in fact, bigger than Elter Water.

TOP, LEFT
Beatrix Potter's love of the Lake District found expression in generous donations to the National Trust and exhibitions devoted to her life and work have become major attractions throughout Lakeland .

TOP, RIGHT
These ramblers at Glenridding, at the southern end of Ullswater, are on one of the hundreds of miles of paths which cross-cross the Lake District .

ABOVE
The River Brathay, rising near Pike O' Blisco in the Langdale Pikes, tumbles over rocks or runs smoothly between trees and meadows on its way down to Windermere. Here, it passes under a stone bridge at Clappersgate, south of Ambleside.

in the 1760s, publishing his *Journal of a Visit to the Lakes* the year before Wordsworth was born.

William Gilpin's account of his visit to Lakeland, which Wordsworth much admired, was published in 1786. This was three years before the French Revolution, which the young Wordsworth greeted with such enthusiasm:

'Bliss was it in that dawn to be alive,
But to be young was very Heaven!'
Wordsworth spent two years in France just after the Revolution and would probably have stayed longer but for the war which broke out between Britain and France in 1793. This was the year in which he began publishing his poems, which included ones set in the Lake District. Although Wordsworth returned to the region of his birth several times in the 1790s, most of the decade was spent with his sister, Dorothy, in the West of England, where he soon gathered round him a group of people, including Samuel Taylor Coleridge and Robert Southey, who were to be lifelong friends.

By the time William Wordsworth returned to the Lake District permanently in 1799, he was already an acknowledged poet. With Dorothy, he settled into Dove Cottage on the outskirts of Grasmere. Here, in 1802, he married Mary Hutchinson, who was to bear him three children at Dove Cottage, and here Wordsworth dedicated himself to poetry, living rather frugally on a small allowance. Soon, the Wordsworths had gathered round themselves a group of friends and admirers, all dedicated to a life of writing poetry. The tag 'Lake Poets' was first attached to Wordsworth and his friends, especially Coleridge and Southey, in a rather derogatory style by the literary magazine, the Edinburgh Review, in 1817. It was not long, however, before an admiration for the celebrated Lake Poets was a main reason for bringing increasing numbers of visitors to the Lake District as the 19th century wore on.

For the young Wordsworth, poetry did not by itself provide a sufficient income for his growing family and in 1810 he turned travel writer by providing an introduction to a book called *Select Views in Cumberland*. In 1835 Wordsworth published an expanded version of his introduction called Guide Through the Lakes. It was a best-seller.

By this time, popular interest in the previously neglected wild country of Cumberland and Westmorland had grown rapidly. Artists of the stature of Turner and Constable, though the latter did not find the region to his liking, had visited and painted many views of the scenery. Jane Austen made a proposed visit to the Lakes a matter of excitement for Elizabeth Bennet in *Pride and Prejudice*.

People of a more outdoor inclination climbed its fells and wrote about their experiences, thus creating a fashion for the Lakes among 'people of sensibility and culture', as Wordsworth called them. Among the visitors were Keats, who climbed Skiddaw; Shelley, who arrived with his young bride Harriet to walk over the fells near Ambleside; De Quincey who arrived, aged 18, as a confirmed worshipper of Wordsworth and stayed for many years; Dickens who climbed Carrock Fell; and Tennyson, who visited his friend James Spedding at Mirehouse, Bassenthwaite, where he was inspired to write the scene of King Arthur's funeral voyage on a barge and the throwing of Excalibur into the lake. Later in the century, the celebrated art critic, John Ruskin, made his home at Brantwood on Coniston Water; after him came such famous writers as Beatrix Potter, Sir Hugh Walpole and Arthur Ransome.

The growth of an affluent society in the industrial cities of the north of England brought a different kind of visitor, many of whom built holiday homes along the more accessible lakes. It also brought grave threats to the serenity of the mountainous Eden in the form of railway entrepreneurs seeking to establish railway lines through Buttermere and the Ennerdale valley and the Manchester Corporation, hard-pressed to provide more urban amenities for the new industrial towns, attempting to turn the lakes into water reservoirs.

Wordsworth fought hard against the intrusion of the railways into the Lake District, fearing the horrors likely to be inflicted on its quiet valleys by 'the Advance of the Ten Thousand'; he could be said to have won the battle in that the railway, apart from lines built originally to serve west Cumbria's mining interests, from Broughton in Furness to Coniston and from Pentrith to Cockermouth, has never penetrated further into the heart of the Lake District than the Windermere terminus of the branch line from Oxenholme, opened in 1847.

Fortunately, the Lakes had many strong-voiced champions, who early on realised that the Lake District was an unique national treasure which needed to be preserved from the ravages of commercial exploitation. One such was Canon Hardwicke Rawnsley, vicar of Crosthwaite, who was one of the founders of the National Trust. Having marshalled the support of many national figures, including Carlyle and Ruskin, Canon Rawnlsey and two enthusiastic companions, Octavia Hill and Robert Hunter, Solicitor to the Post Office, proposed the formation of a National Trust to preserve traditional ways of life in Britain.

The Trust, whose full name was National Trust for Places of Historic Interest or Natural Beauty, came into being in 1895. It quickly grew to be a power in the protection of the English countryside.

One of the National Trust's early purchases, made in 1902, was land along the shore of Derwent Water in the Lake District. Today, the National Trust is one of Lakeland's largest landowners, owning or holding on lease some 140,000 acres, along with many lakes and tarns, farms, cottages and houses, including the house in which William Wordsworth was born in Cockermouth and the house at Near Sawrey where Beatrix Potter, a strong supporter of the Trust, wrote and illustrated her wonderful children's stories.

In 1951 the Lake District National Park, the country's largest, was created. This is a planning authority, not a landowner, and is responsible for the care and administration of some 866 square miles of land stretching from the west coast of Cumbria to the A6 highway and M6 motorway. Within its borders are sixteen lakes, of which Windermere is the largest and Elter Water the smallest, many tarns, four mountains reaching over 3000 feet (923 metres) - Scafell Pike, the highest mountain in England, Scafell, Helvyllyn and Skiddaw - and the high passes which separate them, as well as many acres of the most beautiful country in the land.

Though this most beautiful and unique part of England is more protected today than ever before, those who care for it must constantly be on their guard against those who would develop its commercial aspects on grounds of 'public benefit'. More tourist accommodation, more entertainment amenities and the development of power boating on the lakes are just some of the threats that have been kept at bay. Perhaps the greatest danger is simply the huge numbers of visitors who unintentionally wear out mountain paths, destroy stone walls, and leave litter over the countryside.

Over the years the protectors of this beautiful countryside have held their own and, despite the inevitable overcrowding of the most popular areas, the character of the Lake District has been preserved. It will not be in jeopardy as long as the twelve million visitors a year show the goodwill and common sense to look after the landscapes they enjoy.

OPPOSITE
The River Brathay, after leaving Elter Water, flows rapidly down through a wooded landscape, falling over the rocks of Skelwith Force, a particularly memorable sight when the river is in full spate. Once the river nears Windermere, all is calmness again. At sunset, when this picture was taken, the scene can be magical, with the evening colours reflected in the quiet waters.

The Way to The Lakes

ABOVE
The River Kent, flowing through Kendal from its source on the north-eastern fells, reaches the sea at Grange over Sands. Here, away from the grey stone buildings of the centre of Kendal, the river gives the 'auld grey town' a pleasantly tranquil atmosphere.

LEFT
Sizergh Castle, south of Kendal, was built as a defensive stronghold against raiders from north of the Border. Its handsome peel tower remains a striking feature of the castle, which is now in the caring ownership of the National Trust, one of the Lake District's most important landowners.

The most popular approach to the Lake District is through Kendal, in the valley of the River Kent. This is a green countryside of undulating hills which make a satisfying overture to the dramatic landscapes of the lakes which lie a few miles to the west.

Kendal, which was the largest town in the old county of Westmorland, lies just outside the Lake District National Park. It has a long history going back to the Romans who established a camp, called Alauna, or Alavna, by the River Kent, just south of the present-day town. During the 14th century Kendal grew in importance as a wool town, thanks to the arrival of a group of Flemish weavers in 1331, and many mills, using the water power of the river, sprang up along its banks. In the 19th century, water power was also used at a nearby gunpowder factory which provided explosives for the various mining ventures in the region.

Kendal, whose grey limestone and slate buildings have earned it the name 'auld grey town', rewards close attention. Many of its older buildings are grouped around the Town Hall in the main street, which is known as Stricklandgate at its northern end and Highgate and Kirkland to the south. One of the unusual features of this long thoroughfare - once a main route north to the Scottish border - is the number of courtyards which lead off it, most of them built to house workers in the wool industry.

The M6 motorway, in taking away the heavy traffic which used to thunder through Kendal, has allowed the town to develop a more attractive industry: tourism. It has a Heritage Centre and a fine Museum of Lakeland Life and Industry. The latter is housed in the stables of Abbot Hall, an 18th-century mansion which is now Kendal's main art gallery, where several paintings by the artist George Romney, who was apprenticed in the town, are on view. Romney is also commemorated in the 13th-century parish church, Holy Trinity in Kirkland, which also contains the family chapel of the Parr family.

Outside the centre of Kendal, on the east bank of the Kent, rise the battlemented ruins of a once-splendid Norman castle, birthplace of Catherine Parr, who was Henry VIII's sixth and last wife.

Just a short drive away out of Kendal south along the A6 are two fine houses which make rewarding visits for travellers not too impatient to reach the lakes. First, $3^{1}/_{2}$ miles south of Kendal, is Sizergh Castle, a National Trust property. It is a splendid peel tower dating back to the 14th century and enlarged in Tudor times. Its fine Stuart furnishings and decor provide a vivid picture of the life of well-off Tudors and Stuarts, able to live in comfort without that fear of attack from north of the Border which had made the building of fortified towers so important a century before. Sizergh also has a splendid terraced garden with a pond and a limestone rock garden planted with plants from the Lake District mountains.

A mile and a half south of Sizergh Castle is Levens Hall, a great Elizabethan mansion set in 100 acres of parkland through which flows the River Kent. Like Sizergh, Levens Hall was built in the 14th century as a fortified tower. Its gardens, designed by a Frenchman early in the 18th century, include some of the finest yew topiary work in

Britain. Goats and deer roam in Levens Hall's deer park and to satisfy the modern demand for entertainment at country houses the owners have installed steam traction vehicles, a merry-go-round for children and a display of steam-driven models for all ages.

Both houses are open to visitors all summer – that is, from April to October. These are the months which see the majority of Lakeland's visitors come to the region. It is safe to say that for most visitors to Kendal and its great houses the real goal is the Lake District National Park. Just 8 miles from Kendal, north-west along the A591, or a little further away via the A5074, if you have been visiting Sizergh or Levens Hall, is Windermere, largest of the lakes.

Many visitors heading north-west from Kendal to the Lake District National Park make straight for Windermere, ignoring the

quiet farming country to the north of the town, where the Kentmere Valley and Longsleddale, both within the Lake District National Park boundary, reach up into the north-east corner of the Lake District. While the valleys do not have a great deal to offer motorists, for walkers this is delightfully quiet and peaceful country, with well-marked paths to take them across the fells to the

north of the Kentmere Valley via the Nan Bield Pass to Small Water and Haweswater or to High Street.

The access point for narrow Longsleddale is Garnett Bridge, off the A6. This dale, watered by the River Sprint, remains very much a private place, apparently little changed over the generations. There are old stone-built farmhouses set in a patchwork of

fields and a maze of lanes, few of them sign-posted, to them. On either side, the fells rise steeply. When it rains, the poet Norman Nicholson once wrote, 'water pours down gill after gill till the dale looks like a street of terraced houses with roof gutters all burst'.

Where the road ends, at the highest farm in the valley, there is a track heading from the east side of the valley to Harter Fell and Gatescarth Pass, with Haweswater beyond; the path once linked Longsleddale to Mardale Green, Haweswater's drowned village.

FAR LEFT
Among the attractive features of Sizergh Castle are the beautiful gardens which surround it. They were designed and laid out in the 18th century by the ancestors of the Strickland family who still live there. The handsome terrace has steps leading down to the gardens, including a lake and a fine limestone rock garden, planted with many Lake District plants.

LEFT, ABOVE
Levens Hall, like nearby Sizergh Castle, was built as a defensive peel tower in the 14th century. Also like Sizergh, Levens Hall was turned from a defensive tower to a splendid mansion in Elizabethan times. Today, its fine topiary garden, based on box, holly and yew and here photographed in glorious spring-time dress, is just one of numerous attractions which make Levens Hall a popular place for visitors.

LEFT, BELOW
The start of a hound trail on the fells near Brigsteer, south-west of Kendal. Hound-trailing, in which the hounds follow a scent (or trail) laid in a circular course, has a proud history in the Lake District and is a popular part of the programme at Lakeland sports days. Trails are held in many parts of the Lake District between March and October, which means that many visitors to the Lake District are able to enjoy watching them.

ABOVE
The southern end of Windermere, photographed from Gummers How, above the A592 which skirts the eastern shore of the lake. A curve of the River Leven can be seen in the centre of the picture. The many sailing boats on the lake are reminders that Windermere is one of the most popular of the lakes for boating, with the jetties of sailing schools jutting out into the water.

Around Windermere

Windermere, the longest of the lakes - and, in summer, the busiest - stretches for ten and a half miles from Newby Bridge in the south to Waterhead, near Ambleside in the north. For the best view of the lake, most visitors make for Orrest Head, rising up behind Windermere town; it is just a 20-minute walk up to the viewpoint at the top from a point near the railway station in Windermere, and it is well worth the effort, for the views are very fine indeed.

The lake's main centre of activity is on the east shore, at Windermere, the terminus of the only railway line into the Lake District, and Bowness-on-Windermere, the lakeside resort. Together, the two towns make up the largest urban area in the Lake District National Park, with many hotels and pubs, shops, restaurants and places of entertainment.

There is a Steamboat Museum at the north end of the town and, in Bowness, steamer piers from which summertime boat services leave for lake trips, ensuring that many visitors, without some sort of craft of their own, still find entertainment on the water as well as beside it.

Their lake steamer will take them past Belle Isle in the centre of the lake up to the top of the lake at Waterhead or down to Lakeside at its southern end, past crowds of sailing boats, power boats and expensive cabin cruisers, apparently moored in every bay and inlet. At Lakeside, the boats of several sailing schools provide many a colourful scene on the lake under the lee of the Cartmel Fells. Windermere is one of only five lakes on which it is permitted to launch boats; the others are Coniston Water, Derwent Water, Thirlmere and Ullswater. Only on Derwent Water, Ullswater and

Windermere are power boats permitted and only on Windermere can they be driven at over 10 miles per hour.

The most interesting feature of the privately-owned Belle Isle, set in the lake opposite Bowness and its lively marina, is the large, entirely round house, 54 feet (16.5 metres) in diameter and with a classical portico its only projecting bit, built in 1774 by Thomas English, a Nottingham merchant. The house can be seen from various angles from steamers passing Belle Isle.

Once out of the centre of built-up Windermere/Bowness - something which can be very slow to achieve at the height of summer - visitors find that much of the lake shore of Windermere is relatively uninhabited and very peaceful. On the eastern shores of Windermere, large houses set in landscaped gardens - they would call them villas on the Italian lakes - sit half-hidden on wooded slopes. On this shore, $1^{1}/_{2}$ miles north of Windermere on the road to Ambleside, is the splendid National Park Visitor Centre at Brockhole, one of Cumbria's most popular tourist spots.

The much more heavily wooded western side of Windermere is quite free of motor traffic for much of its length. This is the best side for quiet, lakeside strolls, with the longest clear stretch of pathway running north from the chain ferry terminal for three and a half miles up to Wray Castle, which is not really a castle, but a 19th-century mansion built in medieval style for a Liverpool surgeon; the sixteen-year-old Beatrix Potter had her first Lake District holiday here when her parents hired the building.

The chain ferry gives car drivers wanting to avoid a long drive round Windermere a quick way across the lake; it operates all year round between The Nab, south of Bowness and Ferry House on the western shore. There is a good view to be had from the ferry of Belle Isle's round house.

One of the roads from the ferry's landing stage on the western shore climbs along the southern end of Claife Heights to Near Sawrey and Hill Top Farm, one of the most popular places to visit in the Lake District because the farm was for many years the home of the celebrated author Beatrix Potter.

Hill Top is a simple cottage, kept by the

National Trust with the same loving care they devote to their great mansions, with many of the bits and pieces of furniture, pottery, china, curtains and carpets which Miss Potter put into the illustrations of her books still in place and instantly recognizable by the thousands of children and their parents who come here every year. Six of Beatrix Potter's books, including the tales of Tom Kitten, Jemima Puddleduck and Pigling Bland, were set in Hill Top, while views of the countryside around, which Miss Potter, as Mrs William Heelis, farmed for many years, appear in many more.

Beatrix Potter was encouraged to publish her first book by Canon Rawnsley, founder of the National Trust, and she herself was a great patron of the Trust and its work. With

royalties from Peter Rabbit and subsequent books she bought farms, fourteen of which she bequeathed to the National Trust with some 6000 acres of land.

Once married and settled in the Lake District, Beatrix Potter virtually gave up writing, following a second successful career as farmer, landowner and well-known breeder of Herdwick sheep, the small, hardy breed of the Lake District. It is not surprising that included in her bequest to the National Trust was her flock of Herdwicks. High country sheep farming has always been hard in the Lake District, so Beatrix Potter would not doubt be delighted to know that the National Trust is dedicated to its role as sheep farmer in the Lake District, where its tenants work with many thousands of the

Herdwick sheep, or the Swaledale-Herdwick cross.

Walkers may get an inkling of why Beatrix Potter so loved this gentle, rolling hill country, where descendants of Mrs Heelis' prize-winning sheep still graze, by walking over Claife Heights along one of several footpaths and bridleways – perhaps after a drink and a bite to eat at the National Trust-owned Tower Bank Arms pub just a step from the gate of Hill Top. A very fine walk up Claife Heights runs north from opposite the Tower Bank Arms, climbing up through large rock outcrops to Moss Eccles Tarn, fringed with reeds, beech trees and rhododendrons and home to several kinds of water bird. If the walk is at the end of May, walkers should see plenty of lambs on the fells above High Sawrey, for they are traditionally put out on the fells at this time, having been born from mid-April.

A short distance from Near Sawrey lies Esthwaite Water, a small lake to which Wordsworth often walked when he was at school in Hawkshead. This lake was the scene of the drowning of a local schoolmaster, a tragedy which Wordsworth never forgot, even including it in *The Prelude*.

William Wordsworth is, of course, the other great writer associated with the part of the Lake District centred on Windermere. Although the direct route to 'Wordsworth Country' is north along the eastern side of Windermere to Ambleside, there is also a fine drive from Sawrey to Ambleside, Rydal Water and Grasmere, approaching Ambleside across two rivers, the Brathay and the Rothay, near whose confluence, just above the northern end of Windermere, the Romans built two forts at a place they called Galava. Although the Romans made no attempt to settle the Lake District area, it was important to them strategically and they built numerous forts to guard their roads which linked England's coasts with the interior.

The Brathay has its source on Pike o' Blisco in the Langdale Pikes and the Rothay flows south from Thirlmere towards Windermere, through Grasmere and Rydal Water. The valleys of both rivers are delightful with flourishing deciduous trees and green meadows. A particularly charming place on the Brathay is Elter Water, a small shallow lake which, like many of the lakes, is gradually silting up and on whose reed-filled shores there is an abundance of water birds such as duck, grebes, mergansers and swans. In summer, bird watchers and walkers throng the village of Elterwater, which once housed a gunpowder works, but which is especially valued today for its Britannia pub on the tiny village green.

There are two impressive waterfalls – called 'forces' in the Lake District – in this area, both easy walks from the road. Due south of Elterwater, Colwith Force joins the valleys of Great Langdale and Little Langdale. The force drops a total of 50 feet (15 metres) in a series of mini rapids and a 15-foot (4.5-metre) drop. On the Brathay, where it flows out of Elter Water, is Skelwith Force, not a very high waterfall but one which is particularly dramatic after rain when the water cascades tumultuously over rocks under overhanging trees.

Following the Brathay downstream to its meeting place with the Rothay, where the road turns up towards Ambleside, one could take time to check the truth of the story which says that the char and trout of Windermere swim upstream to the confluence, at which point the char swim up the Brathay to breed and the trout turn up the Rothay.

Ambleside is a busy town, filled to bursting point in summer with tourist traffic, which the local council has vainly tried to order via a series of one-way traffic systems, and with many parties of walkers and climbers, who can hire their climbing equipment at various specialist suppliers in the town. Ambleside has a solid, grey character with a Victorian atmosphere, its main features including St Mary's Church, built in the Gothic style by George Gilbert Scott in 1854, and the Market Hall of 1863. The church is the scene of an annual rush-bearing ceremony, held on the first Saturday in July. These ceremonies, held in just a few north of England villages, including Grasmere, are survivals of a time when most churches had bare earth floors, over which rushes were scattered for warmth and cleanliness.

Another amusing building, which looks like a folly but was in fact a summer house, is Bridge House, built over Stock Ghyll by the main car park. All that remains of the once

imposing Ambleside Hall, Bridge House is now the National Trust's oldest information centre and smallest shop.

Among Ambleside's more famous residents was Harriet Martineau, writer and traveller, who built herself an Italian-style villa, The Knoll, where she lived for thirty years, entertaining fellow writers like George Eliot, Charlotte Brontë and Ralph Waldo Emerson.

South of the town along a busy road is Waterhead, where is the northern ferry terminal for the Windermere lake steamers. It was the opening of this pier in 1845 which led to Ambleside's expansion as a tourist centre. Also near here is the National Trust's Stagshaw Garden, with its fine show of rhododendrons and azaleas in springtime.

From Ambleside there are various delightful and easy walks and car rides. One of the most popular walks climbs steeply up the valley of Stock Beck to Stock Ghyll Force, a waterfall in a lovely setting of trees and ferns which cascades a total of some 90 feet (27 metres) over rocks into a pool.

The road from Ambleside up the Stock Gill valley climbs up to the Kirkstone Pass, at 1489 feet (454 metres) the highest pass in the Lake District. The ancient inn at the top was at one time a meeting place for brigands and highwaymen. There are fine views of Wansfell from here. Descending the pass back to Windermere by the A592 to Troutbeck, along a winding road through hillside farms, gives the traveller the delightful surprise of Troutbeck itself, built on a slope off the road and containing over a dozen 17th- and 18th-century farm buildings. Townend, at the southern end of the village, is a fine 17th-century yeoman farmer's house, miraculously retaining its original character, making it a fine setting for its collection of domestic implements, furniture and old farm vehicles and implements. The house's wool barn, on the other side of the road, still has its original spinning gallery. The home of one family, the Brownes, who lived here from the time the house was built in about 1626 until 1943, Townend is now a National Trust property and is open in the summer months.

The most popular tourist route out of Ambleside is the one north-west out of the town (on the A591) leading to the idyllic lakes of Rydal Water and Grasmere. These two secluded and beautiful stretches of water are the essence of Lake District Romanticism and are closely associated with the Lake Poets.

The road to Rydal Water winds its way through wooded countryside full of charm and as the little reed-fringed lake bursts into view it fulfils all expectations. The tree-clad fells rising all round it, the small islets at its centre, the watery reflections make one instantly think of the poetry of William Wordsworth, murmuring with him
'There was a time when meadow, grove and stream
The earth, and every common sight,
To me did seem
Apparelled in celestial light,
The glory and the freshness of a dream.'
Wordsworth lived in this lovely place, at Rydal Mount, a large house looking out over Rydal Water and Loughrigg Fell beyond, from 1813 until his death in 1850.

Today, Rydal Mount is a pilgrimage centre for lovers of poetry and is furnished with much of Wordsworth's personal furniture and belongings. Below the house is a field, filled with daffodils in spring - though not the ones that inspired his famous poem - which the poet bought in order to build his own house there if the lease on Rydal Mount was terminated. He named it Dora's Field after his favourite daughter, Dora.

Rydal Water was also the home for a time of Thomas de Quincey and Coleridge's son, Hartley, both of whom lived in Nab Cottage, on the northern shore of the lake. At the water's edge, close to the village, look for a low rock, hidden among trees, known as the Poet's Seat.

One of the best viewing points of both Rydal Water and Grasmere is easily accessible from Rydal, reached either by walking along the lake or from the car park at its western end. This walking track leads to Loughrigg Terrace, below Loughrigg Fell.

From here on the bracken-covered slopes there is a superb view of Grasmere, with Helm Crag beyond.

The A591 leaves Rydal Water at its eastern end and turns towards Grasmere village, the southern end of which is called Town End. This was where Wordsworth and his sister Dorothy first settled in 1799 in a cottage, once an inn, and now called Dove Cottage. In 1802 he married Mary Hutchinson and settled down to the most creative years of his life as a poet, writing such poems as the famous daffodils sonnet, 'I Wandered Lonely as a Cloud...', 'To the Cuckoo' and *The Prelude.*

Grasmere is another small lake, just a little larger than Rydal Water, and still with plenty of fish, which Wordsworth often went out in his boat to catch. Perhaps it was while sitting quietly in his boat on the rippling water waiting for a fish to bite that Wordsworth thought of the lines in one of his poems:

> '...if unholy deeds
> Ravage the world, tranquility
> is here!'

Every year, Wordsworth's first home in Grasmere, now owned and maintained by the Wordsworth Trust, receives thousands of visitors, led round the confined quarters by a guide. Next door, in a converted barn, is the Wordsworth Museum which displays some of Wordsworth's manuscripts and possessions and gives a clear and interesting exposition of the Romantic Movement.

Three of Wordsworth's children, John, Dora and Thomas, were born here and when the cottage became too small to hold them they moved to Allan Bank at the foot of Helm Crag and then to the Old Parsonage, opposite the church of St Oswald, which is built on the banks of the Rothay in Grasmere.

The Old Parsonage was cold and damp and two of Wordsworth's children, Thomas and Catherine, sickened and died during

ABOVE
*Rydal Water, near which William Wordsworth spent
the latter half of his life, is a gem of a lake. The still,
reed-edged waters lie in a hollow under Nab Scar to the
north and Loughrigg Fell to the south. It is a peaceful
place – except perhaps at the height of summer.*

RIGHT
*One of the finest views of Rydal Water, from the path to
Loughrigg Terrace, is achieved after a short climb
through woods. The rooftops of Rydal village can be
seen among the trees.*

OPPOSITE, ABOVE
*The dining room at Rydal Mount, dominated by a
portrait of the poet, still retains some of the furnishings
used by Wordsworth and his family.*

OPPOSITE, BELOW
*Wordsworth rented Rydal Mount; to ensure that he
would never have to leave this lovely place, he bought a
field below the house where he could build a house of his
own, if need be. Today the field, known as Dora's Field
after his daughter, is alive with daffodils in spring.*

their tenancy. To add to Wordsworth's unhappiness the new tenant of Dove Cottage, where he had spent happy and productive years, chopped down the orchard and neglected the garden that Wordsworth and his wife had so carefully nurtured. The tenant was his friend Thomas de Quincey, author of *Confessions of an English Opium Eater*, whose habits hardly endeared him to the conservative villagers.

In living at Grasmere and writing his guide book to the Lakes, Wordsworth started a fashion among the well-off, some of whom built splendid houses in local stone in Grasmere. This urbanisation has give the village a special character. With its fine main street, complete with a pleasant village green, tree-lined streets and spacious houses, it is has more the atmosphere of a health spa than a Lakeland town. The popularity of the place has ensured that there are good hotels, restaurants and shops and also the

disadvantage that in summer it is overcrowded and car parking can become a problem, especially during the period of the Grasmere Sports and rush-bearing ceremony in August. The latter is centred on the 14th-century St Oswald's Church and is accompanied by street processions and other festivities.

Grasmere's Sports are the biggest of the Lakeland sports, annual sporting occasions held all over the Lake District during the summer. The events begin with the Penrith Show in July and end with the Wasdale Show and Wigton Horse Sales in October. In between are historic events like the Carlisle Great Fair, the Egremont Crab Fair and the Patterdale Sheep Dog Trials as well as shows and sports in several more of Lakeland's bigger towns. At Grasmere's Sports visitors can mingle with several thousand others, watching a great variety of events, including the traditional Cumberland and

Westermorland wrestling. Championships for this style of wrestling, thought to have been introduced into this part of England by the Norsemen, are a feature of many of the summer shows and games of Lakeland.

In the south-east corner of St Oswald's churchyard in Grasmere are the graves of several members of the Wordsworth family, making the quiet ground a place of pilgrimage. Wordsworth planted in 1819 the yew tree which stands near his grave, shared with his wife, Mary, who died in 1859. Nearby are the graves of Dorothy Wordsworth and three of the Wordsworth children, Dora, Catherine and Thomas. The

John Wordsworth commemorated on a stone nearby was William's brother, who died at sea in 1805.

William Wordsworth and his sister Dorothy were great walkers, discovering many of the beauties of their Lake District home on foot. One walk which they probably knew well - certainly Thomas de Quincy did, for he described it in his writings - is to remote Easedale Tarn, resting in a glacier-carved basin below Tarn Crag. The steep, two-mile walk to the tarn along the course of Easedale Beck, starts from Easedale Lane where it crosses Goody Bridge in Grasmere.

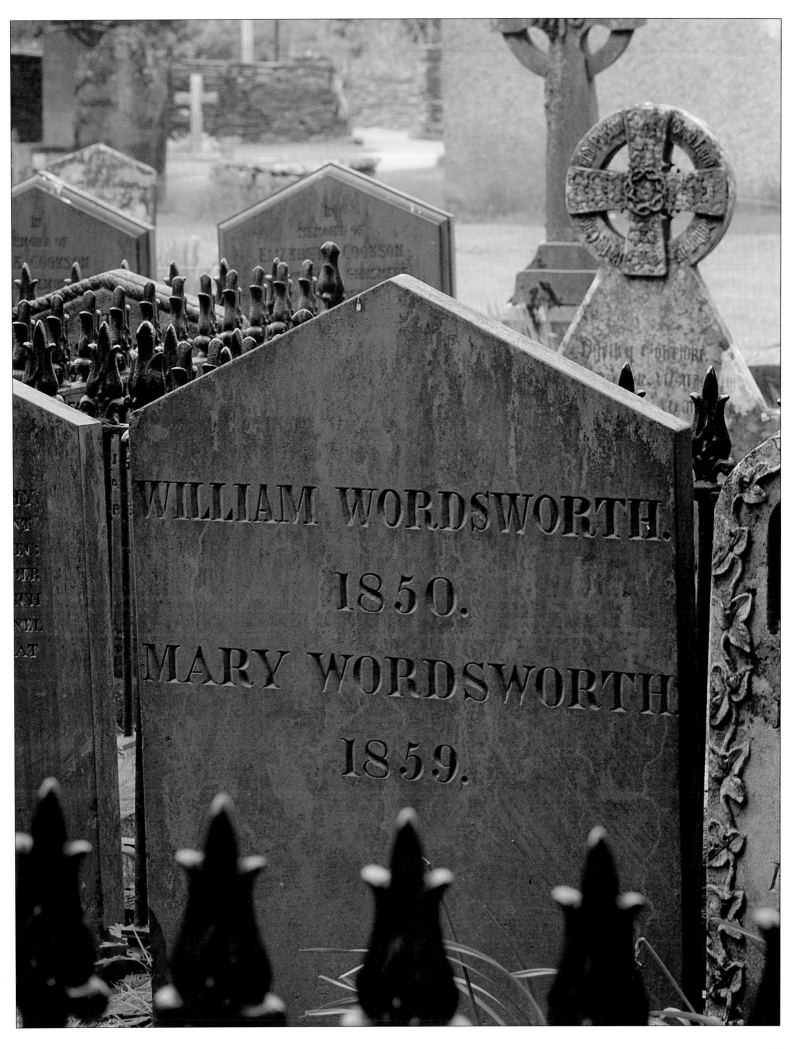

Coniston Water & the Surrounding Countryside

oniston Water, 6 miles by road south-west of Ambleside, lies between the Grizedale Forest, which separates it from the Windermere valley, and Coniston Fells, which rise to the Old Man of Coniston, 2631 feet (802 metres) above sea level. It is the third longest of Lakeland's lakes, stretching virtually in a straight line for 5½ miles - which makes it an ideal sheet of water for attempting water speed records. It

was on Coniston Water that Donald Campbell set a world water speed record of 209.35 miles per hour in 1959, and it was on Coniston Water that he died in 1967 attempting to better his record.

Now the best-known boat on Coniston Water is not Donald Campbell's Bluebird, most of which still lies, with Donald Campbell's body, in the depths of the lake, but the National Trust's steam yacht *Gondola*.

This elegant craft operated on the lake from 1859 to just before the Second World War; John Ruskin used it to cross from his house Brantwood on the eastern shore to Coniston village on the other side. The National Trust bought *Gondola*, restored it to its original style and elegance, and now uses it for a regular steamer service in the summer months, starting from Coniston and calling at piers at Park-a-Moor at the south-east corner of

Coniston Water and at Brantwood.

For a brief period the village of Coniston, about half a mile inland from the lake's western shore and originally a mining village, achieved world fame as Donald Campbell's headquarters. Today all that remains of the Campbell connection is a memorial in the village and a small collection of mementoes in the Ruskin Museum, next to the information centre. John Ruskin, who chose to be buried here rather than in Westminster Abbey, also has a memorial in Coniston village, a fine stone cross, made from stone from Tilberthwaite, over his grave in the churchyard.

Coniston may seem a quiet, even rather nondescript place, a popular rendezvous for climbers and walkers ascending the Coniston Fells, but it has a long and interesting history behind it.

ABOVE
Bought by the National Trust in 1976 and beautifully restored and renovated, the steam yacht Gondola *takes up to 86 passengers in opulent comfort on scheduled sailings up and down Coniston Water in summer. One of its stops is Brantwood Pier, from where John Ruskin would use the yacht to cross from his house to Coniston village. At that time there were two steam yachts on Coniston, both of them built by the Furness Railway Company in 1859.*

LEFT
The cattle standing peacefully in the water by the shore of Coniston Water are evidence of the rural nature of much of the land round this long, straight lake. Once the woods on Coniston Fells, behind Coniston village, sounded to the voices of iron smelters and charcoal burners and, later, briefly, the lake echoed to the fierce sound of the engine of Donald Campbell's Bluebird. *Today, both are silent, with most sounds coming from sailing boats or the National Trust's* Gondola.

RIGHT
John Ruskin, who lived at Brantwood on the eastern shore of Coniston from 1871 to 1900, thought that this view of the Old Man of Coniston and Coniston Fells from his house was one of the best in the world ·

For centuries, a valuable mining industry was established here, mining the copper ore found in the area. There was even a railway from Coniston down to Broughton in Furness; though it closed in 1958, the line of the track still exists. Before the railway, the Walna Scar Road, clearly marked on the Ordnance Survey maps running across Coniston Fells above the west side of Coniston Water and one of the oldest roads in the Lake District, carried for more than a thousand years pack ponies laden with copper ore from Coniston to the coast. Today, walkers reach the road from a clearly sign-posted road running south of the centre of the village, treading a walk followed before them by generations of shepherds, pedlars, traders and wool merchants.

From the Walna Scar Road are paths offering easy climbs to the Old Man of Coniston, a popular ascent since Victorian times. As on many other fells, the well-marked trails are gradually being eroded as the numbers of walkers increase and repairs are constantly in progress. From the summit there are splendid views over the pretty Duddon Valley, a favourite walk for Wordsworth, the river estuaries of Morecambe Bay to the south and the high fells to the north.

Back at lake level, there is a lovely, very quiet walk along the western shore at Torver Back Common. There are few spots at lake level which offer uninterrupted views of Coniston Water, though there is one particularly good view of the lake from its head, from where the water seems to stretch away far into the distance. Wordsworth liked this view, though his other favourite view, across the lake with the Old Man of Coniston rising behind, was from near Brantwood.

Brantwood, on the eastern shore at the northern end of Coniston Water, was just a cottage when John Ruskin bought it in 1871. Much enlarged over the years, and surrounded by gardens which Ruskin steadily extended to 500 acres, this was Ruskin's home until his death in 1900. Art critic, artist, educational theorist and social reformer, Ruskin was a champion of the movement to preserve the Lake District as he was of other causes, such as that of the painter J. M. W. Turner. At Brantwood he devoted himself to filling the house with his collection of pictures, including many great works by Turner, and objets d'art. He also spent a great deal of time making sensitive and highly professional drawings of Lake District subjects. When Brantwood's contents were auctioned by Ruskin's heirs, much of his work was saved by an admirer, John Howard Whitehouse, founder of Bembridge School on the Isle of Wight, who collected the

LEFT
Brantwood was little more than a cottage, famous for its views, when John Ruskin bought it in 1871. Over the years he enlarged the house considerably and also added to the land which surrounded it. Today, Brantwood and its grounds, which includes a three-mile nature trail and the stone seat from which Ruskin used to admire the view, is a popular stopping place on the tourist trail through Lakeland.

BELOW
The view towards the southern end of Coniston Water from Ruskin's dining room at Brantwood. The seven lancet windows are thought to represent The Seven Lamps of Architecture, *one of the books which helped establish Ruskin as the leading art critic of his day. While he lived there, Ruskin filled Brantwood with paintings, including many works by J. M. W. Turner, books and works of art. Although much of the contents of the house was sold after Ruskin's death, much has survived, making Brantwood a high point of any visit to the Lake District.*

many paintings and drawings which are now in the school's possession.

Visitors to Brantwood, which is open in the summer months, find that Ruskin's presence is still strong. There is a large collection of his watercolours, many of his books and art treasures, and a good collection of the house's original furniture. Outside, in the woods and gardens, walks and a nature trail have been laid out. There are also the fine views across the lake which Ruskin claimed were the best in Cumberland; visitors can judge the claim for themselves from a stone seat once used by John Ruskin.

Near the entrance to Brantwood is a more recent acknowledgement of another lover of the Lake District; this is the gallery dedicated to the work of Alfred Wainwright, who spent his life walking and keeping illustrated notebooks of his routes over the Lake District fells. Done purely as a labour of

love, his books were eventually published by the Westmoreland Gazette, and finally appeared in hardback, illustrated versions produced by a London publisher, thus giving Wainwright world renown, including some fame as a television star, at the end of his long life. The gallery contains the printing press on which these unique works were first printed, as well as originals of his work and some of his possessions, including his tweed jacket, pipe and camera.

Another writer to have been inspired by the beauties of Coniston Water was Arthur Ransome, who lived near Coniston from 1930 to 1967 and set *Swallows and Amazons* in the area: 'Wildcat Island' of the book was really Peel Island, down towards the southern end of the lake.

North of Coniston, the country offers much of interest to the visitor, whether walking or driving. A walk which has been

ABOVE
At the lake shore of Ruskin's house, Brantwood, is a stone jetty and tiny harbour where Ruskin moored a boat. In the background, clouds shroud the peak of Coniston Old Man. John Ruskin was an indefatigable explorer of the topographical features of the Lake District landscape. Not only did he study the flora and fauna of the region, but he also made detailed studies of geological formations. Small details were as important to him as the grand, panoramic scene, and he bequeathed to posterity an unrivalled collection of Lakeland studies.

popular from Victorian times combines the Old Man of Coniston with a walk up the Yewdale Beck valley to the north. This pretty little valley, through which the A593 runs towards Ambleside, includes, a mile north of Coniston Village, Yew Tree Farm, one of the oldest existing farmhouses built after the pacification of the Border in the time of James I when farmers began to feel safe from Border raiders.

The new age of law and order and the

acceptance of land tenure by existing farmers encouraged the building of larger, more permanent buildings of which Yew Tree Farm and Townend at Troutbeck are good examples. As in most farms of this type, the living quarters of Yew Tree Farm are separated from the working farm buildings and the house has a 'spinning gallery' where the women would spin and dry the wool which provided both revenue for the farm and the basis of the once very important Lake

Hawkshead, on its southern edge, was once an important market town and centre of the wool trade. It was the village where William Wordsworth went to school after his mother died and before he went to Cambridge. The grammar school is still there, near Hawkshead's handsome church, with the desk on which young Wordsworth carved his name and a windowsill with his brother John's name. Today, the school is open as a museum and much of the atmosphere of Wordsworth's time still haunts the place. This is also true of Hawkshead itself, which is fairly traffic-free because a large car park has been built on the edge of the village. It is a delightful place in which to stroll peacefully in the narrow alleyways and courtyards and among the timber-framed houses and well-maintained shops and cafés with their pleasant architecture and abundant window boxes and flower baskets.

The village first came into being as a wool centre within the estate of Furness Abbey. The monks built the church on its grassy knoll; despite being rebuilt in the 15th century, its rounded arches have a Norman feeling. From the church there is a fine view over the village and to distant Helvellyn, the Kirkstone Pass and Wansfell. Hawkshead Courthouse, built in the 15th century as part of the manorial holdings of Furness Abbey, is now owned by the National Trust and can be visited in the summer months: ask at the National Trust shop in The Square for the key.

The biggest attraction in Hawkshead today is the Beatrix Potter Gallery in Main Street. The building was once the office of Beatrix Potter's husband William Heelis who was a solicitor. In its rooms, largely unaltered since Mr Heelis' time, the National Trust mounts an exhibition of Beatrix Potter's original illustrations for her books; the exhibition is changed annually.

Nearby, are more memories of William Wordsworth in Ann Tyson's Cottage, home of the family with whom Wordsworth lived while at school in Hawkshead. North of the town is a gateway to Hawkshead Hall, a fine house built by the monks but subsequently demolished.

South of Hawkshead, much of the land between Windermere and Coniston Water is moor, fell and forest, with the Forestry

District wool trade.

Near the farm the Yewdale Beck makes a sharp bend up to High Tilberthwaite and the Tilberthwaite Gill and Falls which, with the Tilberthwaite Fells above, provided so many Victorians with the romantic and picturesque scenery for which they visited the Lake District. There are numerous well-marked paths over these fells, just as there are, on the other side of the A593, to a famous Lake District beauty spot here, Tarn Hows, a small tarn made early this century by damming a stream so that two small pools merged into one. The National Trust is the careful and thoughtful owner of this picture postcard-perfect spot, having half-bought and half-inherited it from its previous owner, Beatrix Potter; to see it at its best, however, it is wise to avoid holiday times.

In fact, much of the area to the north of Coniston Water is enchanting countryside, with hilly farms and narrow valleys.

Commission's carefully tended plantation, Grizedale Forest, between Coniston Water and Esthwaite Water, offering a great contrast to the park-like loveliness of much of the countryside further north. The Forestry Commission has laid out five forest walks, beginning from the Grizedale Visitor and Wildlife Centre in Grizedale village, one of which follows the Silurian Way to Carron Crag, at 1030 feet (317 metres) the highest point in the valley. Near the Visitor and Wildlife Centre is the Theatre in the Forest, which has a regular programme of concerts, film shows, plays and lectures. Both buildings give the impression of having been reached through a fairytale forest - Little Red Riding Hood, perhaps? - far from urban life, but in fact they are only 3 miles south-west of Hawkshead.

To the south of Coniston Water and Windermere the land slopes gently down to the sea at Morecambe Bay. Though not all part of the National Park, this is an interesting area for those who have the time to visit it, for it offers a great contrast to the mountains and lakes. Among the several roads leading south, the A590 from Windermere goes through the small hillside village of Lindale where a cast-iron obelisk reminds passersby that 'Iron Mad' John Wilkinson, who lived here for a time, was the owner of the ironworks near Haverthwaite

LEFT
Tarn Hows, a picture postcard-pretty little stretch of water to the north of Coniston Water just off the road to Hawkshead, was not around for William Wordsworth to write poetry about, for it came into being only at the beginning of this century when the farmer who owned the land joined two smaller tarns together to make a reservoir. What he made has become the Lake District's most popular tarn, visited by an estimated three-quarters of a million people every year. Tarn Hows was one of the beauty spots of the Lake District bought by Mrs William Heelis (Beatrix Potter). She sold half of it at cost to the National Trust and bequeathed the Trust the remainder.

FAR LEFT
Tarn Hows in late summer, with the rich glow of drying bracken making a striking foreground for the views of distant Wetherlam and Langdale. Tarn Hows is so popular in late summer that its owners, the National Trust, have had to institute a one-way system for motorists to avoid traffic jams. They have also completed an excellent walk right round the tarn.

LEFT
Beauty of a different sort at Tilberthwaite Gill, north-west of Coniston. The old slate quarries and levels which once provided work and incomes for many on these fells are now deserted, leaving gauntly picturesque ruins scattered across the land. Tilberthwaite Gill, a secluded valley off the Yewdale Beck valley, was a popular walk for Victorian visitors to the Lake District, and the stone for John Ruskin's memorial in Coniston came from here.

which cast pieces of the first iron bridge in Britain, erected in Ironbridge in Shropshire.

Down on the coast is Grange-over-Sands, a quiet seaside resort near which are the cliffs of Humphrey Head Point, the last vestige of the mountain ranges of the Lake District. A couple of miles inland of Grange-over-Sands is Cartmel, a very attractive village of interest for its priory church founded early in the 12th century for the Augustinian order. All that is left of the priory of which the church was a part is the gatehouse, now owned by the National Trust and leased out as a picture gallery.

Near Cartmel lies another of the great houses of the peninsula, Holker Hall, once a home of the dukes of Devonshire. Most of it was destroyed by fire in 1871 and what is visible today is largely the Victorian house, lavishly re-built in Elizabethan style, which replaced it. The house is finely furnished throughout and includes some excellent paintings. Among its outside attractions are a 23-acre garden and the Lakeland Motor Museum, with a fascinating collection of motor vehicles, two- and four-wheeled, a reconstructed pre-war garage and a full-size replica of Donald Campbell's record-breaking Bluebird.

To the west across Cartmel Sands is the Furness peninsula, with Duddon Sands, the estuary of the River Duddon, on its western shore. The southern tip of this large peninsula is just within the Lake District National Park. The peninsula is largely industrial along its coast, with Barrow in Furness at its southern tip at the head of a harbour ideal for shipping.

The quick way back to the Lake District proper from here is via the A590, with Furness Abbey, signposted off the road north of Barrow in Furness, well worth visiting. The sandstone abbey, now an impressive ruin, was one of the great abbeys of England and was built by Savigny monks about 1130. By the time of Henry VIII it was the second richest Cistercian house in the country (Fountains in Yorkshire was the richest),

holding great tracts of land in Cumberland and Westmorland as well as Lancashire and the Pennines. Bow Bridge, half a mile from the abbey, is a handsome three-arched packhorse bridge which served one of the abbey's granges.

Further north on the A590, Ulverston offers a good reason for stopping in the form of the small Laurel and Hardy Museum, commemorating the life and career of Stan Laurel, of the famous Laurel and Hardy film comedy partnership, who was born in the town.

While the A590 will take the traveller back to the southern end of Windermere, the A5092, off the A590 at Greenodd, offers a fine

ABOVE, LEFT
William Wordsworth was a pupil at this grammar school in Hawkshead from 1779 until he went up to Cambridge in 1787. Like other boys of his time, he carved his initials in his desk, which can be seen in the school building, now a museum

ABOVE, RIGHT
Hawkshead Methodist Church sits next to a teashop in the midst of a group of white-rendered houses typical of the centre of Hawkshead

alternative back into the Lake District via the Duddon Valley, the road for which heads north off the A595 at Duddon Bridge, past Broughton in Furness, a pretty village whose market square indicates its former importance as a market town.

The little-visited Duddon Valley was a favourite of Wordsworth's, largely because of the picturesque and even dramatic course taken by the River Duddon down it. He wrote thirty-four sonnets about the river and its valley, brought together under the title The River Duddon. Wordsworth's usual approach to the valley was from its northern end, of course, from the Wrynose Pass, the source of the river, which flows down the valley with the Old Man of Coniston the highest peak above its eastern bank.

A particularly picturesque part of the Duddon Valley is the section between Seathwaite Fells, on the eastern bank, and Harter Fell, on the western side. There has been a major afforestation programme in the Duddon Valley since the 1930s, and its present-day appearance at this point would probably seem quite alien to Wordsworth, who protested vigorously at the introduction

of the larch into the Lake District at the end of the 18th century, remarking that acres of it 'can grow up into nothing but deformity'. He would surely not have liked the conifers that now reach up Harter Fell to a height of 1500 feet (457 metres).

There is a car park at Birks Bridge, an excellent example of a pack-horse bridge about 2 miles north of Seathwaite, and well-

marked walks along the river and up the fells. From here the road runs parallel to the river which is bordered by woods along its west bank. From Seathwaite there is a short but interesting walk to Wallowbarrow Crag which rises sheer above the woods.

ABOVE, LEFT
Grizedale Forest is the Forestry Commission's largest area of planting in the Lake District, which it began planting in 1937. Today, there is a Visitor and Wildlife Centre, a fine Theatre in the Forest and forest 'sculptures', using local materials, set in many places along the forest walks.

ABOVE
Furness Abbey, imposing in life as the second most powerful Cistercian abbey in England, remains impressive today as a ruin.

The Western Lakes

The lakes of the western side of the Lake District, separated from those of the centre and east by the great massif of the high fells, have valleys that open out towards the green and flat coastal fringe of Cumbria. Apart from the many tarns and reservoirs which hide in basins on the fells, there are five main lakes in this area.

On the eastern edge of the area are Buttermere, Crummock Water and Loweswater, a chain of small, very lovely lakes, all now owned by the National Trust. From the northern end of Crummock Water the River Cocker flows north to join the Derwent at Cockermouth. Ennerdale Water and Wast Water lie to the south. The first three lakes are easily reached by car from the central Lake District, either from their southern end via Borrowdale and the Honister Pass or from Keswick in the north,

either (the long way) via the Whinlatter Pass and the valley of the Cocker, or on a direct road from Keswick to Buttermere village. Another way in, giving the visitor a wonderful contrast as the valley of the Cocker narrows to enclose the lakes, is from Cockermouth. Ennerdale Water and Wast Water can be reached by road only from the west, for the country between the two groups of lakes is high fell country, dominated in the east by Great Gable.

The three lakes in the north of the area are all quiet spots, where visitors come for the fishing and boating and for the pleasant walks round the lakes and up on to the fells. A succinct summing up of the three would be to say that Loweswater is immensely lovely, like something in a Turner watercolour, Crummock Water's attraction is wilder, bleaker, and Buttermere offers an exhilarating combination of the two. The most popular of the three is Buttermere, a particularly lovely lake, just $1^{1}/_{4}$ miles long, set against particularly impressive fells, dominated by the slopes of Red Pike, High Stile and High Crag to the south, the colours of which change with the light and the seasons.

The most popular way into Buttermere is by way of the Honister Pass from Borrowdale and Seatoller, which has a good National Park Visitor Centre. The 1176-foot (358-metre) Honister Pass, despite its 1-in-4 gradient, is a not particularly demanding route into Buttermere, despite the alarmingly steep-looking scree slopes and the rugged Honister Crags which add to the rather sombre atmosphere of the pass. There is a slate quarry at the top of the pass which may be visited by appointment. From the car park near the quarry buildings there is a relatively easy walk to Fleetwith Pike (2126 feet/648 metres) from which the view down the valley is splendid.

Buttermere, once reached, more than makes up for the Honister Pass. The road passes along the northern side of the lake to reach Buttermere village set round a cross roads between Buttermere and Crummock Water. The village is pretty, with two inns built below the tiny church of St James, built in 1840, and numerous stone-built cottages. There are a few guest houses, and a big car park to cater for all the visitors, most of

whom manage some walking during their visit.

The most popular walk, because it is easy and all on one level, is the one right round the lake, parts of it through pine forest and bracken and even, at one point, through a tunnel in a cliff. Another interesting walk is one of about $2^{1}/_{4}$ miles to Scale Force, at 140 feet (43 metres) the highest waterfall in the Lake District. The Sour Milk Gill waterfalls (not to be confused with the one of the same name in Borrowdale), which cascade 700 feet (213 metres) down from Bleaberry Tarn into Buttermere, offer another walk from Buttermere. They are reached via a lane going south from the church. Beyond the waterfalls, the path becomes the route to Red Pike, from the 2479-foot (755-metre) peak of which are some of the Lake District's finest views, taking in five lakes.

A more difficult walk is to Haystacks, the great wall of crags rising up beyond the head of Buttermere from Warnscale Bottom near Gatesgarth. Less lofty than its neighbours, Haystacks, once the walker is up there, is enormously impressive, which is why it is the fell that Wainwright chose to have his ashes scattered over.

All these walks, apart from Haystacks, are likely to be quite crowded in summer. The visitors are, in fact, following a long-established tradition, for Buttermere as been a popular tourist spot since the beginning of the 19th century. They came in their thousands after one J. Budworth noted in his A Fortnight's Rambles in the Lakes, published in 1795, that the fifteen-year-old Mary Robinson, daughter of the keeper of the Fish Inn, '...looked an angel, and I doubt not she is the reigning lily of the valley'. Mary's later career included innocent marriage to a bigamist and forger who was hanged at Carlisle a year after the wedding, leaving Mary to be delivered of a still-born child. The poet Coleridge wrote up her sad story for the Morning Post, which brought even more visitors to Buttermere, and Wordsworth found room for her in The Prelude: '... the spoiler came and wooed the artless daughter of the hills, and wedded her, in cruel mockery...'. Thomas de Quincey gives a colourful account of the affair, including Coleridge's and Wordsworth's interest in it, in Recollections of the Lakes and

the Lake Poets, and present-day visitors have been reminded of the story by Melvyn Bragg's novel *The Maid of Buttermere*.

Crummock Water, the middle of the chain of three lakes, is also the biggest, being 5 miles long and very deep. Once joined with Buttermere as one stretch of water, Crummock Water is separated from it by low-lying meadows. Surrounding it are range upon range of splendid fell country. The best walk at lake level is on the western shore, because the road is so near Crummock Water on its eastern side.

A more ambitious walk from Crummock Water is up Grasmoor (2791 feet/850 metres), a formidable and massive giant rising along the north side of the lake. This is a difficult climb from the lake shore and has to be outflanked by walking up Gasgale Gill and doubling back to the summit at Force Crag. (Another, entirely different, approach to Grasmoor is from the north, from Braithwaite village on the B5292 Keswick – Cockermouth road and up the Coledale Beck.)

From the summit of Grasmoor there is a splendid view of the fells on the southern side of Buttermere and Crummock Water. The summit is surrounded by steep slopes and cliffs, particularly on the west side and the panorama is exceptional among Lakeland fells views.

Between Crummock Water and Loweswater to the north is a green and undulating landscape of farms and woods dominated by the bulk of Mellbreak to the south. Here, set among the farms, is the village of Loweswater with its cosy old Kirkstile Inn, a gathering place for walkers exploring Loweswater Fell or the reed-fringed edges of the lake and its abundant birdlife. The Kirkstile Inn is also a meeting place for the Melbreak Hunt, one of the six packs which hunt the fox on foot in the Lake District. The Melbreak hunts the fells around Loweswater and Buttermere.

Most of the south side of Loweswater is covered by Holme Wood, a lovely area of mixed woodland, including ash, oak, chestnut, sycamore, elm and birch reaching 900 feet (274 metres) up to below the crags of Burnbank Fell and Carling Knott. Hidden in its heart is Holme Force, a series of cascades on the Holme Beck tumbling through the woods. The force is easily reached from the shoreline path: turn up alongside Holme Beck where the path fords it.

On the north side of Loweswater is bracken-covered Darling Fell, from which there are good views to the heart of Lakeland in one direction and of the coastal plain in the other, including, on a clear day, the Solway Firth and the lowlands of Scotland beyond. Darling Fell is reached by a detour off the fine walk which circles Loweswater.

Flowing out of the northern end of Crummock Water, the River Cocker runs through a fine open valley, Lorton Vale, which also carries minor roads from the three lakes, down to Cockermouth, where the Cocker joins the Derwent. Joining the valley from the east at Lorton is the road down the Whinlatter Pass from Keswick. Two places of interest on the Whinlatter Pass road are the Whinlatter Visitor Centre, run by the Forestry Commission, at the eastern end of the pass, and Spout Force, a 30-foot (9-metre) waterfall, signposted off the road, near the western end. The Forestry Commission owns some 30,000 acres of the Lake District and carries out essential work in re-afforestation and care of the landscape. Though sometimes criticised in the past for its insensitive planting in geometrical patterns, the Commission is now careful to follow where possible the natural contours of the land. The visitor centre explains the work of the commission and provides maps for walks in its Thornthwaite forests nearby.

For motorists wishing to visit the lakes to the south of this part of the Lake District, Cockermouth, despite being north of the Buttermere lakes, and therefore in quite the wrong direction for Ennerdale Water and Wast Water, is, in fact, a good place to aim for first.

Cockermouth, lying just outside the boundary of the Lake District National Park, is the main town in this north-west corner of Cumbria and is best-known today for being the birthplace of William Wordsworth in 1770 and of his sister Dorothy in 1771.

Cockermouth is not a tourist town, leading its own pleasantly quiet life as a market town offering among its attractions some fine antique shops and printsellers. Once famous for its hiring fairs, Cockermouth still has a busy cattle and street market. Monday is market day, when people come

into town from the surrounding area.

The broad and tree-lined Main Street is its busiest thoroughfare. Wordsworth House, a large Georgian house at the western end of Main Street, is where Wordsworth was born. It is now in the care of the National Trust. Seven of its rooms are furnished in the style of the period and contain objects that belonged to Wordsworth and to Robert Southey.

Although Wordsworth did not live there after his mother died in 1778 and he left for school at Hawkshead, Cockermouth seems to have left a strong impression on the poet, for he describes bathing in the river in *The Prelude*. He probably also recalled playing in the grounds of Cockermouth Castle, a redoubt built to withstand the incursions of Robert the Bruce in the 13th century and used later to hold off attacks by Yorkist forces at the time of the Wars of the Roses.

Another son of Cockermouth was Fletcher Christian, the leading mutineer of HMS *Bounty* who ended his days on lonely Pitcairn Island in the South Pacific. Both Christian and Wordsworth attended Cockermouth's grammar school, on the site of which today are some rooms built for All Saints Church, where visitors may see a

ABOVE
In this attractive Georgian house in Cockermouth's Main Street, William Wordsworth was born in 1770. Now in the care of the National Trust, the house is open to the public, with seven rooms furnished in 18th-century style and including some items which once belonged to the poet. The garden where Wordsworth and his three brothers and sister Dorothy played has a terraced walk and slopes down to the River Derwent.

LEFT
Cockermouth has been a market town since the 13th century and parliamentary borough since 1295. It remains a quiet town, outside the bustle of the tourists' Lake District. The tree-lined Main Street, photographed here, is Cockermouth's busiest street.

stained-glass window dedicated to Wordsworth.

With more lakes and tarns and a large section of the coast of Cumbria still to be explored in this area, the visitor's first choice of route out of Cockermouth is likely to be the A5086 south. This skirts the western edge of the National Park on its way down to the coast, with minor roads off it leading to Ennerdale Water. The minor road at Mockerkin, which is good for the Buttermere lakes, also offers an elevated road, with good views to the coast, to Ennerdale Bridge, whose Shepherds Arms pub is important because it is the nearest pub to Ennerdale Water.

Isolated from the central Lake District by a formidable barrier of fells, including Pillar, Steeple and Great Gable dominating the head of its valley, Ennerdale Water is among the remotest of the sixteen main Lakeland lakes, a wild place edged by scree slopes and barren fellsides. There is a minor road to bring people from Ennerdale Bridge to the foot of the lake, but there is no road round the lake itself, which is today a reservoir serving the industries and towns of the Cumbria coast, which means that private boats are forbidden. There has been much afforestation round the lake, with the great Ennerdale conifer forest stretching from halfway along the northern shore of the lake up to the head of the valley, down which flows the River Liza. The Forestry Commission has set three trails through the forest, the Smithy Beck Trail, the Nine Becks Walk and the Liza Path, of varying lengths. Youth hostels and mountain rescue posts dot the map here, indicating the area's popularity with walkers and climbers.

The river that flows from the foot of Ennerdale Water is the Ehen, which eventually reaches the Irish Sea near Sellafield, British Nuclear Fuel's great power station.

Sellafield, the world's first nuclear power station, opened in 1956, when it was called Windscale. Today, the latter name applies just to part of the original site, for the nuclear power station has grown enormously over the years and now covers 700 acres, including Calder Hall power station (a local name: the ruins of Calder Abbey, founded in the 12th century and later part of the possessions of

Furness Abbey, lie near Calder Bridge at the foot of the fell road south from Ennerdale Bridge) and the world's most important nuclear reprocessing centre. It is one of the most visited places in Cumbria, some 200,000 people coming to its futuristic-style visitor centre every year. The centre offers simulations of a nuclear chain reaction and the inside of a nuclear reactor in operation; there are also many computer- and

cannot hope to compete with the beauties and pleasures of the lakes.

Before the railway opened up Liverpool, Whitehaven was the second biggest port in England, shipping out locally-mined coal to Ireland and Europe, and taking in tobacco from the American colonies. Still with an appreciable amount of 18th-century architecture in the old centre as well as a fine museum and art gallery, it is probably the

Three views of Ennerdale Water. Although Wordsworth knew the lake well, and set his poem 'The Brothers' nearby, he probably would not recognize much of the surrounding fells now, for there has been considerable Forestry Commission planting since the 1930s.

LEFT
The eastern end of Ennerdale Water, looking towards Pillar and Scout Fell ·

TOP
Looking towards Ennerdale Water from the north, where sheep and cattle graze on low-lying pasture

ABOVE
Cottages at Mireside, on the northern shore of the lake, photographed from the site of the old Angler's Inn

electronically-operated games and displays.

The coast of Cumbria north of Sellafield is without a great deal of interest to the casual visitor, though it has been important for its ports and mines since Roman times.

Egremont's main sight is the ruin of its old castle, dominated by a gatehouse and three arched windows. Whitehaven, Workington and Maryport are still busy places, with their share of museums and places to visit, but most interesting of the three towns. Book lovers could happily spend hours browsing among the thousands of books at Moon's Bookshop in Roper Street, one of the biggest second-hand bookshops in Cumbria.

From the main road south of Sellafield several roads branch off in the direction of Wast Water, the deepest and, to the minds of many Lakeland admirers, the most austere of all the lakes.

The first impression for visitors reaching the lake road at Wasdale Hall is a striking one, for the eastern side of the three-mile-long lake is walled by screes which slither down precipitously to the dark waters of the lake. The wild character of the lake is further dramatised when the south-west wind piles up the waters of the lake in waves which dash north-east towards Great Gable, Scafell Pike and the high fells.

The south-western part of the lake shore is wooded and green but soon the rocky fells close in, with Middle Fell and Yewbarrow crowding down towards the water. The upper end of Wast Water opens into a valley, its pastures surrounded by the typical drystone walls of the Lake District, dominated by Kirk Fell, Lingmell and Great Gable, with the valleys between them providing access. Wasdale Head village is small with stone houses; the Wasdale Head Hotel provides for the many walkers and

climbers setting off for or returning from Great Gable, at the heart of the highest part of England.

People who have driven to Wast Water must turn back south, making either for Gosforth on the A595 or for Eskdale Green and the roads back to Ambleside, via the steep and rugged Hard Knott and Wrynose passes, or down to Ravenglass on the coast via a road down the valley of the River Esk, or over Birker Fell to Ulpha and then to Coniston in the north or Broughton in Furness in the south.

Hidden in the featureless moorland south of the Birker Fell road is the strangely desolate Devoke Water, considered to be a

The Screes of Wast Water, making a wall up to 1983 feet (604.5 metres) high on the south-east side of the lake. One of the Lake District's more exhilarating ridge walks, with ever-changing views, including Wast Water on one side and Burnmoor Tarn on the other, follows the top line of The Screes, reaching its highest point at Illgill Head.

LEFT

The south-western end of Wast Water is deceptively open on the north shore; the ground is flat and covered with grass and bracken. Middle Fell, rising steeply ahead, closes the gap between the north shore and the steep, austere screes of the south-eastern side of the lake and makes a notable gateway to the head of the lake.

tarn, though in area it is bigger than Elter Water, smallest of the lakes. Devoke Water, in its bleak setting, has known many centuries of occupation by man, for it was Neolithic farmers who cleared the forest which once surrounded it; burial mounds, stone circles and other remains on the fells here are thought to date back to the Bronze Age.

Legend has it that there was even a city here once, at Barnscar about a mile south-west of the tarn. To find Devoke Water, watch out on the Birker Fell road for a signpost pointing north to Stanley Ghyll; on the other side of the road a short track goes south-east to Devoke Water.

Eskdale, in contrast to the country round

FAR LEFT

The head of Wast Water in Wasdale. Wasdale Head, at the centre of the broad valley, is a favourite gathering place for climbers, for from here, valleys cut ways up into the high fells. To the north runs Mosedale with the Black Sail Pass making a way between Yewbarrow and Kirkfell. To the north-east, the valley of the Lingmell Beck leads up to Styhead Pass between Great Gable and Lingmell and has paths to Scafell Pike.

Devoke Water, is a pleasantly mellow valley watered by the meandering River Esk and offering numerous interesting and attractive walks. An easy walk a mile south from Dalegarth Station at the head of the dale is to Stanley Ghyll Force, set amidst old woodland and luxuriant ferns.

Boot, a tiny village near Dalegarth Station, has a good inn, an old stone bridge and an ancient corn mill restored to working order by the then Cumberland County Council in 1972. Many people who walk through the interesting exhibition in the mill will have reached it, not by car, but the splendid miniature Ravenglass and Eskdale Railway, affectionately called 'L'al Ratty', whose terminus, after a 7-mile journey up from Ravenglass, is at Dalegarth Station.

The line was opened in 1875 to serve the Nab Gill iron-ore mines above Boot but the mining company went broke and the railway had a precarious career as a tourist line until it closed in 1913. Opened and closed again in the coming decades, the line seemed doomed until it was bought by a group of local railway enthusiasts in 1960. Today it is a popular tourist attraction, open all year round with modern miniature open-topped and enclosed carriages pulled by steam or diesel engines.

The train journey back down to Ravenglass, the only coastal village in the National Park, takes 40 minutes. Though its

fine natural harbour made Ravenglass a very busy port from Roman times, the harbour silted up and Ravenglass's industries and market closed down. Most people now come to this quiet town because of the railway, which has its headquarters and a museum in the town. Visitors to Ravenglass at the end of June should keep an eye out for competitors in the gruelling Three Peaks Race, as the village is on the race route, which contestants have to sail and walk, taking in the three high peaks of Britain, Snowdon, Scafell Pike and Ben Nevis.

Muncaster Castle, east of the town, and Muncaster Mill to the north, are both worth visits. The castle, still owned by the Pennington family who have lived in it since the 13th century, has an impressive peel tower with fine views of Eskdale and the western fells. The house is open to visitors and includes a splendid octagonal galleried library and a drawing room with a barrel-vaulted ceiling; works of art include four portraits by Reynolds and sculpture by Canova. The garden surrounding Muncaster Castle are justly famous; a nature trail has been laid out in the grounds.

Muncaster Mill has its own station on the Ravenglass and Eskdale Railway. It is a watermill which operated from the mid-15th century until 1961. Now owned by the railway company, it has been carefully restored, is working again milling flour (which can be bought at the mill) and is well worth a visit.

TOP
Ravenglass, viewed across the Esk estuary. Once the site of a Roman fort, Glannaventa, and later a busy port and market town and even a haven for smugglers, Ravenglass today is a quiet place. The Ravenglass Gullery and Nature Reserve on the north side of the estuary, managed by Cumbria County Council, has England's largest colony of black headed gulls.

FAR LEFT
A miniature engine and carriages of the Ravenglass and Eskdale Railway come to a halt at Muncaster Mill, a working watermill restored by its owner, the railway company.

LEFT
Muncaster Castle began life as a defensive peel tower, providing a refuge against raiders coming up the estuary. Over the centuries its owners, the Pennington family, gradually enlarged it, culminating in a rebuilding as a splendid mansion around 1800. King Henry VI, taking refuge in the castle after a defeat in 1461, gave the Lord of Muncaster a curious green glass enamelled bowl, known as 'The Luck of Muncaster', which is still one of the castle's treasures.

The North-East Lakes

Three lakes, Thirlmere, Ullswater and Haweswater, as well as many tarns, including Brothers Water and Blea Water, are among the attractions of the northeast corner of the Lake District, but it is Helvellyn that is the magnet for so many visitors to the area.

At 3118 feet (950 metres), Helvellyn is the third highest of the Lake District high peaks and it dominates the north-east section of Lakeland, both physically and spiritually. It is spectacular in itself, especially if viewed along the famous Striding Edge, and the views from the top are also splendid. Said to be the most climbed mountain in England, it is certainly the most popular in the Lake District, for it offers both easy and challenging routes.

The least taxing approaches to Helvellyn are from the west side, which is bordered by the waters of Thirlmere, with one of the most popular starting points being from near Wythburn Church at the southern end of Thirlmere. More adventurous climbers start from Patterdale or Glenridding, at the south-western end of Ullswater, their ways converging at Red Tarn where there are two possible ascents, along either Swirral Edge or Striding Edge. The latter is the one most climbers aspire to for its knife-edge drama and sheer views to the north towards Great Dodd and to the south are irresistible. Despite its vertiginous appearance, Striding Edge is not as dangerous or demanding as it looks and generations of climbers have marked a well-worn path along the Edge and another one just below the crest, a boon on windy days.

Wordsworth took his friend Samuel Taylor Coleridge up Helvellyn in 1799 and Coleridge climbed it frequently thereafter, often simply because it was on the route from his house in Keswick to Wordsworth's in Grasmere. In *A Walk Around the Lakes*, Hunter Davies describes how Coleridge once climbed Helvellyn by moonlight, arriving at Grasmere with enough breath left to recite the latest

lines of his poem 'Christabel' to Wordsworth (clad in a dressing gown because he had already retired to bed when Coleridge arrived) while Dorothy cooked him a chop, presumably to sustain him on the walk back home.

Coleridge and some friends once climbed Helvellyn and had a picnic and let off fireworks at the top, which is so flat and grassy that an aeroplane could land there - which one did in 1926, a feat commemorated on a memorial at the summit. The whole of

ABOVE
Walkers dwarfed by the immensity of their surroundings on Striding Edge, the most exciting way up to Helvellyn. Provided walkers are wearing proper footwear, there is little to worry about on Striding Edge, despite its reputation, much of which derives from stories of accidents there. One such was an incident in 1804 , when one Charles Gough fell to his death, his faithful little terrier keeping vigil by his dead master for three months before they were found. Both Wordsworth and Sir Walter Scott wrote poems about this incident.

RIGHT
The Helvellyn range seen from Grisedale, a valley south-west of Patterdale. The Helvellyn range was another of Wainright's chosen ridge walks, from Grisedale Pass in the south to Threlkeld in the north and taking in Dollywaggon Pike, Helvellyn, Stybarrow Dodd and Great Dodd.

the Helvellyn range makes a superb ridge walk, one of the finest in the Lake District; many walkers choose to start at the southern end at Dollywaggon Pike by Grisedale Tarn and walk to Helvellyn and on along the summits to Raise (2889 feet/880 metres), Stybarrow Dodd (2756 feet/840 metres), Watsons Dodd (2584 feet/788 metres) and Great Dodd (2807 feet/855 metres).

Thirlmere, stretching for $3\frac{1}{2}$ miles along the western edge of this great range of peaks, was once two lakes, linked by a bridge in a strikingly pretty valley much admired by Victorian artists and writers. Then along came the Manchester Corporation, seeking to merge the two lakes into one great reservoir

to provide water for the fast-growing industrial cities of the north of England. The public outcry was enormous and involved such major national figures as Thomas Carlyle, John Ruskin and two of the founders of what would become the National Trust, Octavia Hill and Canon Rawnsley.

The Corporation won the battle and began work on making their reservoir in 1879, starting off by building two roads round Thirlmere, the eastern one of which is now the A591. Soon, the ancient hamlet of Wythburn, on the eastern shore, and Armboth House, on the western side and reputed to be the haunt of phantoms, had disappeared beneath the waters of the new

reservoir; Wythburn Church escaped the flood because it was built on higher ground than the rest of the village. Although the conservationists lost the fight, they could be said to have won a longer-term war, for conservation was now a national issue, hastening the formation of the National Trust in 1895, the year after the Thirlmere reservoir was completed. When the Manchester Corporation tried in the 1960s to turn Ullswater into a reservoir as well, they were defeated, despite the support of the Conservative government of the day, by public opinion carefully and more professionally marshalled by much more experienced conservationists.

In recent years, the appearance of the land round Thirlmere has been much improved by the water authorities and the National Park, who have planted trees along its shores, built a lakeshore footpath on the western side and made access easier for cars. No power boats are permitted on Thirlmere, and a permit is needed for small, non-powered craft, for which there is a launching place at Armboth.

There is still no direct way for motor traffic across the fells between Thirlmere and Ullswater, though there are many miles of tracks and paths for walkers. Motorists must join the A66 north of Thirlmere to reach Ullswater, or approach it from Ambleside by

the Kirkstone Pass.

Motorists making for Ullswater from Thirlmere by the A66 are all too often unaware that their route is skirting the southern edge of a splendidly wild and little visited part of the Lake District National Park. It includes the mass of Skiddaw Forest, dominated by Skiddaw, Lakeland's fourth highest mountain, in the west; 2847-foot (867-metre) Blencathra (Saddleback), also in the Lake District's top ten high mountains, and reached by intrepid walkers from Scales, on the A66, via Scales Fell and Sharp Edge; and, almost on the northern boundary of the National Park, Caldbeck, an attractive village of stone-built houses made prosperous in the

19th century by the rich mineral resources, including lead and copper, of Carrock Fell.

Because his wool-manufacturer friend, John Woodcock Graves, wrote a poem about him which was later set to a very catchy tune by William Metcalfe, a local Caldbeck huntsman called John Peel has become renowned wherever hunting is a sport.

John Peel (1776-1854) lived and died in Caldbeck and is buried in St Kentigern's churchyard there (near the grave of Mrs Mary Harrison who, as Mary Robinson, became famous as the Maid of Buttermere). In his lifetime, John Peel was locally famous, hunting the foxes of the fells with his own pack of hounds, on foot on the higher fells

and on horseback on the lower, less hilly farmland.

Today, hunting is still very much a part of the life of the local people, who support three hunts, two of them mounted, in the area. Caldbeck's pack which hunts on foot is the Blencathra, one of six fell packs in the Lake District which follow the Cumbrian style of fell-hunting on foot from autumn through to spring. Today's packs have full-time huntsmen and are much more professionally organized than in the days when John Peel, having decided the day was right for hunting - and most days were in his calendar - would don his 'coat so grey' (not 'gay': it was a traditional wool coat made from the undyed wool of Herdwick sheep and woven in Caldbeck) and call out other farmers with the sound of his horn.

For the Lakeland visitor heading south again from Caldbeck, the minor road south at Hesket Newmarket for Mungrisdale (both of which are neatly attractive places, highly suitable picture postcards subjects) offers an opportunity to get a real feel of John Peel hunting country. There is a lonely, bleak little

PAGE 54
Thirlmere, a serene and lovely presence glimpsed through trees on the shoreline, shows no hint of the controversy which surrounded its creation, when an ancient road and hamlet and a lot of land were inundated to turn the lovely lake into a three-mile-long reservoir in 1894 .

PAGE 55
Saddleback, or Blencathra, to give it its ancient name, seen from St John's in the Vale, north of Thirlmere. The mountain rises above the valley of Threlkeld, from where it is relatively easily climbed. There is also an ascent by way of Scales which allows a view of Scales Tarn, set in such a hollow that it is said to reflect the stars at noon.

THIS PAGE, LEFT
Cattle graze in front of the theatrical backdrop of the ruins of Lowther Castle. The castle was designed by Sir Robert Smirke to replace the Lowther family's 13th-century hall which was burnt down in 1720. The castle, completed nearly a century later, was itself reduced to a shell in 1957 when its interior was demolished.

BELOW
Caldbeck Fells photographed from the Uldale – Caldbeck road to their west. While Caldbeck Fells were once the happy hunting ground of John Peel and his hounds, they were also famed for the lead and copper mining carried on there, with such romantically-named places as the Brandygill, Roughtengill and Silvergill mines being worked in the 16th century. Today, sheep-grazing is a more important activity, though the wool industry has not retained its once-important place in the local economy.

tarn, Bowscale Tarn above the River Caldew, to be discovered here. The hamlet of Bowscale is a mile north of Mungrisdale and from a row of cottages there a well-defined path goes on to open fellside and up the valley, crossing a beck before climbing up a natural dam of Ice Age moraine which holds in the dark waters of Bowscale Tarn. The walk to the tarn should take about 30 minutes. Across the valley the view is dominated by the screes of Carrock Fell, at the foot of which there is a road leading up to a mine where wolfram was worked until quite recently. On Carrock Fell's summit are the remains of what was once the largest hill fort in Cumbria. Usually silent and empty, this apparent wilderness, known as 'Back o' Skiddaw', once sounded to the clamour of John Peel's hunting horn and the baying of hounds.

Back on the minor road at Bowscale, it is a short drive south to the A66 and on eastwards to Penrith, an ancient market town now cut off from the Lake District proper by the M6, so that it now seems a gateway to the area rather than part of it. Despite the motorway, Penrith is still plagued by traffic because the A6, long a main route to Scotland, still passes through it. The Romans were here for a time and the Normans built a castle, as protection against the Scots, at the end of the 14th century. The town, which is just five miles from Ullswater, is worth a visit, partly for its Steam Museum and the ruins of its castle, but mostly for its good range of shops and places to eat.

Near Penrith there is some very attractive and peaceful countryside, especially along the broad, green limestone valley of the River Lowther.

Lowther Park, Lowther Castle and Askham, in the Lowther Valley south of Penrith, are all part of the Lowther estate, the largest privately owned estate in the Lake District. Its owner is the Earl of Lonsdale, descendant of the first earl whose patronage, in the form of the job of Distributor of Stamps for Westmorland and, later, for Cumberland as well, gave William Wordsworth financial security in the last decades of his life.

Despite its picturesquely ruined appearance and its setting in the lovely Lowther Park, Lowther Castle dates back only to 1806, having been built to replace a

house destroyed by fire some years earlier. The castle was never finished and was deliberately reduced to a ruin in the 1950s, when the estate was going through a time of great financial difficulty.

Although the castle is not open to the public, largely because its ruins are dangerous, there is a pleasant and easy circular walk in the countryside round it, taking in the hamlets of Helton and Whale and the attractive village of Askham, which gets close to the castle and the two fine avenues of oak trees which lead from it. The Lowther Horse Trials, complete with country fair, are held in the beautiful park which surrounds the castle in August.

Askham is a fine village, its long, broad main street lined with trees and enough greensward to make it a sort of village green. Askham Hall, at the east end of the village, is the present home of the Earl of Lonsdale and the Lowther family.

From Askham it is a short distance by road to Pooley Bridge, at the eastern end of Ullswater, though many Lakeland visitors, before heading for Ullswater and deprived of

a stately home visit at Lowther Castle, choose first to turn north from Pooley Bridge and drive up the Eamont Valley on the A592 to visit the historic house, Dalemain.

This fine medieval country house, with the standard peel tower of the region hidden at its heart and with wings added in the time of the first Queen Elizabeth, now has an impressively symmetrical Georgian facade of pink sandstone. Inside, Dalemain has fine old oak panelling, Chinese hand-painted wallpaper and a priest's hole which provided a hiding place at the time of the Civil War. One of the charms of this fine house is that it is not simply a museum but is still lived in by the Hasell family, who bought it in the 17th century and whose ancestral portraits by such eminent painters as Van Dyck and Zoffany decorate the walls.

Ullswater, $7\frac{1}{2}$ miles long, is the second longest of the Lakeland lakes. Wordsworth once said of this lake of many moods that it was '...upon the whole, the happiest combination of beauty and grandeur which any of the Lakes affords.' It also gave him the theme for one of his most famous of poems,

OPPOSITE

Askham is one of the prettiest villages in the north-east Lake District. Built along the edge of the Lowther river, it is part of the Lowther estate, the largest privately-owned estate in the area. Askham Hall on the edge of the village, now the home of the Lowther family, whose head is the Earl of Lonsdale, dates back to the 15th century. Sir James Lowther, later the first Earl of Lonsdale, employed Wordsworth's father and the Lowther family later proved good patrons of Wordsworth himself.

LEFT

Attractive stone bridges over rivers are a feature of the Lake District landscape. This one spans the River Eamont at Pooley Bridge at the northern end of Ullswater.

BELOW

Dalemain, a fine country mansion with a splendid Georgian facade built round a medieval peel tower, lies in the valley of the Eamont south of Penrith. The house has been the ancestral home of the Hasell family since the mid-17th century and its interior remains of that period rather than the 18th century. The Cumberland and Westmorland Yeomanry Museum is housed at Dalemain, which is open to the public.

'Daffodils', for it was at Gowbarrow Park, on the western side of the lake that he and Dorothy first encountered that magnificent crowd of golden daffodils

> '... tossing their heads in sprightly dance.
> The waves beside them danced; but they
> Outdid the sparkling waves in glee:
> A poet could not but be gay,
> In such a jocund company.'

Gowbarrow Fell, above Gowbarrow Park, offers pleasant and easy walking with quite breathtaking views over Ullswater and away north to Great Mell Fell. The main object of any walk over Gowbarrow Fell must be the waterfalls of the Aira Beck which reaches Ullswater via a wooded rocky gorge at the western edge of Gowbarrow.

Though none of the Lake District waterfalls compare in size and grandeur with the world's great falls, they possess a small and intimate charm which stays long in the memory, Aira Force perhaps more than most.

Aira Force is the waterfall nearest the lake, a silvery stream of water dropping a precipitous 80 feet (24 metres) down a narrow gorge. Two bridges span the gorge, the stone one at the top giving a splendid view down the gorge and making a good watchpoint for the abundant birdlife which inhabits the gorge. Aira Force can be reached from lake level, of course, visitors having been provided with a car park at the foot of Aira Beck.

The main tourist centre at the southern end of Ullswater is Glenridding, once a small mining village and now given over almost completely to the tourist trade. As a main starting point for walks to Helvellyn and around Ullswater, Glenridding has a good National Park information centre, plenty of map shops and a large car park. It is also the southern terminus for the Ullswater steamer

service, based on restored 19th-century steamboats, which operates on the lake in the summer months, with piers at Glenridding, Howtown on the eastern shore, and Pooley Bridge at the top of the lake.

For an especially good view of the Helvellyn peaks and the length of Ullswater, many walkers make for Sheffield Pike, on the western shore of the lake above Glenridding. A good starting point is from the A592, at the point where a sign-posted track goes to the hamlet of Seldom Seen; from Seldom Seen there is a path up Sticks Pass which circles Sheffield Pike.

Like Glenridding, Patterdale village, a couple of miles further south, is of little interest in itself but offers accommodation for walkers, as there is good fell-walking country on either side of Patterdale. For the less adventurous there is a fine walk on the attractive and uncrowded eastern shore of Ullswater, with a lakeside path as far as Howtown, where the road down the eastern side of the lake turns inland to end in the dales on either side of Martindale. There are also relatively easy walks around the fells at

this end of Ullswater, including Place Fell and Hallin Fell, which juts out into the lake below Howtown.

The main road from Ullswater to Windermere, the A592, goes south through Patterdale and the Hartsop valley over the Kirkstone Pass. The ascent up to the pass on the Patterdale side is given considerable interest by Brothers Water in the Hartsop valley. Some say that Brothers Water, not Elter Water, should be Lakeland's sixteenth lake, for it is a fine broad stretch of water set attractively in the well-cultivated Hartsop valley, where stone walls separate the fields and sheep graze peacefully. Low Wood, on the western shore of Brothers Water, is a mixed woodland which has been designated a Site of Special Scientific Interest.

The village of Hartsop, off the A592 just before Brothers Water, has houses with spinning galleries and some attractive stone cottages. There is a car park at the far end of the village, ideal for leaving the car while following one of several clearly-marked walks over the fells here.

The fell country between Brothers Water and Haweswater in the east, dotted with tarns including the lovely Angle Tarn and Hayeswater (both reached by walks from Hartsop), is dominated by a long ridge called High Street. This was the road the Romans pushed across the peaks as part of their main way south from their fort, Brocavum, the

remains of which are near Brougham Castle south of Penrith, to their fort at Galava near Ambleside. In true Roman style, High Street follows a well-defined path more-or-less straight ahead for 10 miles along the ridge, allowing the Roman legions to make safe passage above the savage Celts in their valleys below. The path is thought to have existed before the Romans came to Britain and was certainly used for centuries afterwards, by Vikings, merchants, pack ponies and shepherds. For many years the annual Mardale Shepherds' Meet, a big sporting occasion in the area, was held on the smooth, grassy summit of High Street, the fell at the southern end of the Roman's High Street.

From High Street there are several ways down towards Haweswater, the most easterly of the lakes, especially at its southern end, where is Lakeland's deepest tarn, Blea Water, set below the sheer cliffs which edge High Street and above Mardale. Once a small lake accessible by road from the Lowther valley and renowned for its secluded charm, Haweswater became one of Britain's largest reservoirs when the Manchester Corporation completed damming it in 1940, raising the level of the lake 96 feet (29 metres) and drowning the village of Mardale Green. When the ruins of the village reappeared during the great drought of 1984 people and television crews flocked from miles away to see them.

Haweswater has probably not since had so many visitors at once, partly because to reach it by car one must approach it from the north-east and partly because there is no denying that its role as a reservoir detracts from its charm, especially when the water

level is low and the white edges of the reservoir become apparent.

But the fells around it, lonely and with fine views, are rewarding for walkers who seek in the Lake District places that most visitors ignore

East of Haweswater, where the fells, remote and barren, stretch to the horizon, the River Lowther has its source in a remote valley high on the eastern fells. Here are two ancient religious buildings. West of the village of Shap, on the A6, is Shap Abbey, or the Abbey of St Mary, to give it its original name, which was the last abbey to be built in England, being built for the Order of Premonstratensians at the end of the 12th century. At the Dissolution of the Monasteries in Henry VIII's reign part of the abbey was converted into farms and the rest

OPPOSITE, FAR LEFT
The spinning gallery on this house in Hartsop is a reminder of the time when the woollen industry was of paramount importance to the Lake District economy. Farmers' wives would spin the wool and leave it to dry on these galleries. Much of it would then be sent to towns like Hawkshead or Kendal, where the manufacture of 'Kendal Green' cloth sustained the town's wealth for several centuries.

OPPOSITE, LEFT
Sheep grazing on the fells above Mardale, at the head of Haweswater. The sheep are Swaledales which, with Herdwicks, were the mainstay of the Lake District woollen industry, being tough and able to withstand the rigours of a high country winter. Herdwicks are the tougher of the two breeds, but Swaledales are more prolific and fatten better. Whichever sheep he has, however, the modern Lake District farmer does not, despite government subsidies, have the same incentive as his ancestors to farm sheep.

OPPOSITE, BELOW
Hartsop Dodd reflected in the still surface of Brothers Water. This tarn in Patterdale is said to have acquired its present name from an incident involving the drowning of two brothers. An earlier name for it was Broad Water, probably arising not from the fact that it is almost as wide as it is long, but from a Norse word referring to the ancient road which passed it.

LEFT
Roman legionaries probably knew this view of Hayeswater for it is taken from High Street, used by the Romans to get their troops safely through the wild north-eastern fells of the Lake District. The tarn is set in a deep cove 1383 feet (421.5 metres) above sea level.

was allowed to decay. The evocative ruins, the largest piece of which is a 16th-century tower, are now in the care of English Heriage.

Less than a mile away, across stone-walled fields, is the second religious building here, Keld Chapel. This is a small pre-Reformation chapel, still used occasionally for services, though it now belongs to the National Trust.

Good walks from the southern end of Haweswater include the old pack-horse way to Nan Bield Pass to reach Small Water, linked to Haweswater by a beck which flows into the larger lake under a footbridge, and a walk to Harter Fell via Gatescarth Pass, from which it is possible to follow an old track down to Longsleddale.

OVERLEAF
Although the water level is somewhat low in the Haweswater Reservoir it is not low enough to reveal anything of the drowned village of Mardale Green which, with its old churchyard and 17th-century Dun Bull Inn, famous as the home of the Mardale Shepherds' Meet, disappeared beneath the waters of the new reservoir in the late 1930s.

Around Derwent Water

Two lakes dominate this Lakeland area. To the north is Bassenthwaite Lake – subject of an old schoolboy riddle based on the question 'What is the name of the only lake in the Lake District?' because it is the only one of the major lakes of Lakeland not to be called either 'water' or 'mere' – and further south is Derwent Water, which, apart from being a very lovely lake, is distinctive for being the only one of the major lakes which is more oval in shape than long and narrow, measuring $3\frac{1}{4}$ miles from north to south and nearly $1\frac{1}{4}$ miles across at its widest point. The two lakes are joined by the River Derwent.

The main town of the area is Keswick, built on the alluvial plain between Bassenthwaite Lake and Derwent Water. Like Ambleside, Keswick looks slightly forbidding at first sight because of its stone-built Victorian architecture. It is, in fact, a bustling resort with enough guest houses and B&Bs to accommodate the crowds that fill it in summer. An old market town with a pencil-making industry based on local granite and slate quarrying, Keswick grew in importance as a holiday centre in Victorian times, many thousands of visitors being conveyed there on the Cockermouth, Keswick and Penrith Railway which had originally been built to serve the iron ore industry.

The centre of Keswick is around Market Square and Main Street which is dominated by the Moot Hall, a building with a steep sloping roof and a clock tower in a somewhat Alpine style, which was built in 1813 to replace a 16th-century courthouse. The street level of the building was originally an open market, but the arches were filled in and shops replaced the market stalls. Today, the Moot Hall houses a big National Park information centre.

As well as a theatre, cinema, and three museums, Keswick has a Beatrix Potter 'enterprise', run by the National Trust. Where the Trust's Beatrix Potter Gallery in Hawkshead is concerned with her literary work, Keswick's Beatrix Potter's Lake District, as it is called, emphasises her great achievement in conserving with care and

sensitivity 6000 acres of the Lake District.

Of Keswick's three museums, the most interesting is the Fitzpark Museum, which is Keswick's museum and art gallery combined. It is a traditional-style museum with lots of glass cases housing an esoteric collection of items including a penny-farthing bicycle and a mummified cat. For most visitors, the main subjects of interest are the manuscripts and documents relating to famous writers who lived in the Lake District, including Wordsworth, Coleridge, Southey, de Quincey and Hugh Walpole.

Another of Keswick's museums recalls the days when Cumberland graphite was the raw material of the Cumberland pencil industry, which grew up in the days of Elizabeth I and which continues today, though now using imported graphite. The Cumberland Pencil Museum, near Greta Hall, is one of Lakeland's top tourist attractions. It traces the history of the manufacture of pencils over the years; among its more unusual exhibits are pencils designed for World War II fighter pilots complete with secret maps showing how to escape from enemy territory.

The local railway society runs Keswick's Railway Museum, a small museum with mementos and ephemera of the now defunct Cockermouth, Keswick and Penrith Railway.

There is no museum devoted to the Lake Poets, despite the fact that both Samuel Taylor Coleridge and his brother-in-law, Robert Southey and their families lived at Greta Hall, just out of the centre of present-day Keswick, Southey eventually dying there in 1843. The house, named after the River Greta which flows through Keswick before joining the Derwent just west of the town, is now part of Keswick School and so is not open to the public.

Coleridge and his family moved into Greta Hall in 1800, when Wordsworth was at Dove Cottage and the two men saw a good deal of each other, though, in the end, Coleridge's nonconformism and his use of opium began to get on the nerves of the more conservative and reactionary Wordsworth. Coleridge lived at Greta Hall and then for a

time with Wordsworth at Grasmere. But the Lake District climate did not suit his health and he went to Malta for a time, leaving his wife with the Southey family, before leaving the Lake District for good in 1810. Southey, on the other hand, moved into Greta Hall in 1803 and spent the rest of his life there.

Coleridge was successful, where Wordsworth had not been, in persuading Charles and Mary Lamb to visit him in the Lake District, but was unable to inspire Charles Lamb with his enthusiasm for the region. The Lambs dutifully accompanied Coleridge up to the top of Skiddaw and to the Lodore Falls but were unimpressed,

circle of thirty-eight stones and an inner rectangle of ten stones. Nobody knows exactly why this circle, like Stonehenge but smaller, was built, though its age seems to correspond to the Neolithic or Bronze Ages. Why was it built and why here? Did it have a religious or astronomical significance? One fact that may have some bearing on its construction is that it overlooks some of the highest fells in the Lakes, including Helvellyn, Blencathra and Skiddaw.

Castlerigg is not the only circle in the Lake District; there are others or vestiges of them right across the region. In the country south of Penrith are numerous antiquities, including a circle of sixty-five stones on Heughscar Hill near Askham in the Lowther Valley and the remains of another, from which most of the stones were removed in the 19th century, at Mayburgh Henge near Eamont Bridge; in the south-west of the region, a near-complete circle of fifty-five stones still stands at Swinside near Broughton in Furness.

Archaeologists think that these circles

Charles Lamb agreeing that they were excellent places for romantic tourists, though they made too much spluttering about it.

Southey, poet, historian and biographer and general man of letters, who was Poet Laureate from 1813 (Wordsworth followed him in the role from 1843), was happy working in his library at Greta Hall, finding inspiration in the beauty of the countryside, some very fine views of which he could have all year round from his library window.

Robert Southey is buried in the churchyard of the lovely Crosthwaite parish church, in the north-west part of Keswick, where he had long worshipped; in the church is a white marble monument to the poet, with an inscription written by Wordsworth. The Vicar of Crosthwaite for many years was Canon Rawnsley, co-founder of the National Trust. One of his many purchases in the Lake District was Greta Hall, which he later sold on to Keswick School.

It is safe to assume that Canon Rawnsley would not have cared for the ring road which now passes behind the church, though there are still fine views south to the Derwent Fells, which Coleridge and Southey both loved, from the churchyard.

The country all round Keswick, not just to the south, has many splendid viewpoints. From Castle Head, half a mile south of Keswick, there are unforgettable views over Derwent Water and Bassenthwaite Lake, while 1203-foot (367-metre) Latrigg, a mile to

the north-east, offers even larger panoramas.

There is also, east of Keswick along the B5322, one of the most puzzling sights in the Lake District. This is the prehistoric Castlerigg stone circle, consisting of an outer

probably fulfilled a number of purposes, both religious and practical, and were used as ritual gathering places and as market gathering places by the early Lakeland dwellers who first penetrated the valleys on hunting expeditions armed with the stone axes which they made on the slopes of Langdale.

Mystery has long surrounded the part of Lakeland around Derwent Water, and it is not surprising that during the romantic 19th century the picturesque landscape became an inspiration for many poets and writers. One such was Sir Walter Scott, who used the legend of Castle Rock in *The Bridal of Triermain*. Castle Rock is a crag high up St John's in the Vale, a valley east of Keswick down which the St John's Beck runs from the northern end of Thirlmere to join the Greta. In certain lights the crag looks exactly like a castle with towers and turrets and it was here that Scott located the home of a beautiful but wicked witch and her companions.

Alfred, Lord Tennyson, another great poet of the 19th century, also found inspiration near here. He used to stay with his friend, the writer and patron of the arts James Spedding, who lived at Mirehouse, on the eastern side of Bassenthwaite Lake. According to local legend, it was while he was staying here that Tennyson, who was engaged in turning the epic story of King Arthur into *The Idylls of the King*, conceived the idea of having the dead king transported across a lake on a barge and his sword Excalibur being returned to the waters from which it had sprung.

Mirehouse, a small country house set in attractive gardens with a pretty walk, is open to the public in the summer months. In the elegantly furnished house manuscripts from the hands of Tennyson, Wordsworth and Southey are preserved, and there is some ephemera relating to the Spedding family.

One other writer who made his home in this area must be mentioned: Hugh Walpole, creator of the Herries family, whose wild activities he recounted in a series of highly romantic novels in the 1930s. Walpole chose that Judith Paris, eponymous heroine of one of the novels in his hugely popular Herries Chronicles,

should live at Watendlath, a tiny hamlet of stone houses, on the fell above the southern end of Derwent Water. It is reached by a minor road sign-posted off the B5289 south of the lake and the house in which the fictional Judith Paris 'lived' is marked with a plaque. Watendlath is at the northern end of a small tarn and there are footpaths from here to other tarns on the fells, including remote Dock Tarn and Blea Tarn, both of them involving walks of about a mile from Watendlath.

The Watendlath valley was famous long before Hugh Walpole put Judith Herries there, for near the bottom of this hanging valley the Watendlath Beck tumbles over the Lodore Falls down into the River Derwent in Borrowdale. An over-enthusiastic guide book writer called these falls 'the Niagara of England' in 1829. Visitors today can judge for themselves, for there is an easy footpath to the Falls round behind the Swiss Lodore Hotel on the lake shore. It is a good idea to try to see the Falls after there has been plenty of rain; after dry weather, the Falls are little more than a trickle - certainly not the splendid cascade

PAGE 68, ABOVE
Keswick, at the head of Derwent Water, is an ancient market town with a Victorian air, relic of a major building programme after the Cockermouth – Penrith Railway began bringing visitors in large numbers to the town .

PAGE 68, BELOW
Most of the big stone-built houses on The Headlands in Keswick, built in palatial style for Victorian visitors, are now hotels and guesthouses .

PREVIOUS PAGE
The River Derwent meanders into Derwent Water. The river's 30-mile course takes it from Sprinkling Tarn, beyond Glaramara, through lovely Borrowdale, Derwentwater and Bassenthwaite and past Cockermouth to reach the sea at Workington.

OPPOSITE, ABOVE
Castlerigg Stone Circle, a Neolithic stone circle of some 40 stones, the highest of them seven feet (just over two metres) tall, stands on high ground, with hills and fells all round, in the countryside east of Keswick. It is not the biggest stone circle in Cumbria: Long Meg and Her Daughters near Little Salkeld has 65 'daughter' stones and Long Meg is 12 feet (3.65 metres) high.

OPPOSITE, BELOW
The head of Bassenthwaite Lake. Although the lake looks quite shallow here, it does reach a depth of 70 feet (21 metres) half-way along its length. Sailing boats and rowing boats are permitted on the lake, but not powerboats.

BELOW
Mirehouse, where Tennyson stayed during an inspirational visit to the Lake District

of water that inspired Southey's poem, 'How Does the Water Come Down at Lodore', known to every Victorian schoolchild.

Sir Hugh Walpole himself lived on the western side of Derwent Water, below Cat Bells, a deceptively gentle and low-looking fell which, in fact, offers splendid views. A fine view of Cat Bells itself may be had from the garden terrace of Lingholm, home of Lord Rochdale, who opens his lovely woods and formal gardens to the public in the summer months.

Like Beatrix Potter, who wrote the story of Squirrel Nutkin at Lingholm, Hugh Walpole loved Cat Bells and called Brackenburn, his house there, 'a little paradise'. The house is not open to the public, but nearby Brandelhow Woods, on the shore of the lake, certainly are; this was the first piece of land the National Trust bought in the Lake District, acquiring it in 1902 to ensure public access to the lake shore.

The view from here of Derwent Water, reed-fringed for long stretches, backed by cliffs and craggy fells or well-wooded slopes in other places, and with the Jaws of Borrowdale at the southern end, is enough to

confirm the view of many people that Derwent Water is 'Queen of the Lakes'. There are also four main islands set like stage scenery in the lake, giving extra interest to the circular launch trips round the lake run from Keswick Lakeside throughout the summer.

The largest of the islands, set almost in the centre of Derwent Water, is St Herbert's Island, named after a saintly hermit and disciple of St Cuthbert who lived on it in the 7th century. Little remains of his hermitage apart from a pile of loose stones but with a little imagination it is not difficult to picture the solitary and dedicated life of the monk who, with others on the mainland, were preserving the light of culture and faith at a barbaric time in the history of Western civilization.

Near St Herbert's Island is Rampsholme Island; then, further north and near the eastern shore of the lake is Lord's Island, where the Earl of Derwentwater once had a house; and, near the northern end of the lake, is Derwent Island, where a colony of German miners, brought over to work on the Goldscope mine in 1565, was established. One other island, near the lake's southern end, is an occasional affair for it consists of a tangled mass of vegetation and weeds sometimes pushed to the surface by marsh gas.

The best view of Derwent Water and, according to Ruskin, one of the finest three views in Europe, is from Friar's Crag, a headland on the eastern shore reached by a path from Lakeside car park at Keswick. From here, it is possible to see all four of Derwent Water's main islands and much else besides.

At the southern end of Derwent Water is the broad green valley of Borrowdale, down which the River Derwent flows on its way into Derwent Water, having traced its way down from the high fells between Great Gable and Glaramara.

As the valley rises it becomes narrower, hemmed in by wooded slopes and crags: ideal scenery for romantic artists and poets, many of whom made this one of their most loved parts of the Lake District. In the centre of the valley rises formidable Castle Crag, once a redoubt from which Britons defied the power of the Roman army and now the

perfect viewpoint for a bird's eye view of Borrowdale. Another good balcony from which to get a view of the valley is the Bowder Stone, a relic of the Ice Age when glaciers carved out U-shaped valleys and carried enormous stones in their frozen streams. After the strenuous climb up either viewpoint, most people repair to the nearby village of Grange where a comfortable hotel and small cafe restore weary visitors.

Borrowdale is the perfect gateway to the central high fells and the base from which many people begin climbs to such summits as 2560-foot (780-metre) Glaramara, Great Gable (2949 feet/899 metres) and Fleetwith Pike, beyond the western end of the Honister Pass.

At its upper end, Borrowdale opens up into green farmland hemmed in by steep fells and here are the last villages walkers will come to before beginning their climb into the high fells. Rosthwaite, a little group of stone cottages just off the main road, is the largest of them, and has a good hotel. A well-defined pony track provides a good walk with wonderful views from the village up to Watendlath; the walk should take about an

hour there and back.

Stonethwaite is an isolated village, off to one side of the motor road and Seathwaite is even smaller, reached via an unpaved road off the B5289 just before Seatoller. The B5289 is the road over the Honister Pass to the Buttermere lakes.

Walking the Fells

The central fells – bare, impressive, boulder-strewn slopes broken by jagged crags and sheer precipices – appear on the map as the hub from which the lakes of the Lake District fan out like spokes on a wheel. In this area, south of Derwent Water and the Buttermere lakes, are some of the most photogenic peaks of the Lake District. Even in photographs peaks like the Scafells, the Langdale Pikes, Bow Fell and Great Gable stir the blood and create a tremor of excitement and anxiety. From every summit, other summits can be seen stretching away in every direction and the dizzying views down through the clefts in the mountains are of green valleys and silver lakes and rivers. In cloudy weather the dramatic effect is enhanced by swirling mists and an eerie silence; when there is a break in the clouds the grandeur of the scene is something only ever equalled by the works of the painter Turner in its glory.

All of which stirs the imagination to thoughts of a wild, untamed landscape full of excitements and dangers with arduous scrambling over sliding screes. These are thoughts which arouse, among those who have not walked the fells, fears of being unable to cope with England's wildest mountains.

In reality, Lakeland is one of the most accommodating areas of unspoiled landscape in the world, offering both easy paths for the most timid of walkers and exciting challenges for the most intrepid of rock climbers. Services provided by local authorities ensure that no-one who ventures into the mountains is ever far from help should they be in trouble as a result of some foolhardiness or over-confidence, or of a sudden change in the weather.

Many walkers on the Lake District's fells are holidaymakers without the special equipment of the dedicated walker or mountaineer. In fact, for most fell walkers, essential equipment need consist just of a good pair of stout walking shoes with soles able to prevent slipping, a warm sweater and waterproofs which will keep out sharp winds as well as rain. Unless the walker is going to

be doing nothing more strenuous than the walk round Buttermere or Tarn Hows, people are usually advised not to wear jeans as they are too tight and constricting, while wet denim is a very uncomfortable fabric. Basics for the haversack of a walker planning to be out for several hours should include spare sox and warm head covering, first aid kit (with plasters for blisters), food and drink, torch, compass, and an Ordnance Survey map. A whistle to attract attention is also a good idea; the recognized cry for help is six blasts on the whistle once a minute.

There are those who walk – and even run – the fells in a competitive spirit, determined to conquer all the peaks and summits of over 2500 feet or to make circuits of all the

ABOVE
Walkers silhouetted against the skyline negotiate Windy Gap, Great Gable. From Great Gable's summit there are superb mountain panoramas to be enjoyed, as far as the Isle of Man in one direction and Windermere in another. If the weather is clear, it is possible to see all the great Lakeland peaks, including the Scafells, Skiddaw, Saddleback and Helvellyn.

RIGHT
The remains of the Roman Fort on Hardknott. The fort, on the Eskdale side of Hardknott, was one of the first Roman sites in Britain to be examined in detail and the remains of a large bath-house as well as camp accommodation, a granary and the parade ground have been unearthed. Judging from the fragment of an inscription found in 1964, the fort would seem to have been built in the reign of the Emperor Hadrian.

summits in a particular area, their aim being to achieve athletic success like climbers of the Scottish high peaks or alpine peak 'collectors' in the European Alps. For most people, however, the Lakeland fells are best enjoyed by going easily and steadily and being observant, for in climbs from valley floor to summit, walkers pass through a panorama of English natural life as the flora and fauna change with the height of the landscape.

In rich and fertile valleys like those of the Langdales, or on the lower slopes of fells, the countryside has much in common with the rest of England: beautiful woods and stands of deciduous trees and green meadows providing a home for the meadow pipit, blackbird, ouzel, nuthatch, jay and woodpecker. Around the lakes there is a superb variety of water fowl, including coots, grebe, and duck, including mallards, teal and mergansers. As the land rises, the woods become thinner, much of them having been destroyed for fuel in the time when the Lake

District was being developed as an area for mining and gunpowder-making. The trees on the rising slopes tend to be coniferous, due to generations of planting by the Forestry Commission, but there are also rowan, holly, oak and ash stubbornly hanging on in what is a rocky soil in which erosion has played havoc with fertile top soil. Young tender plants of the kind found in hedgerows and fields have a hard time surviving as the rocky slopes begin and the pervasive bracken, pretty as it is in spring with its fresh green and in autumn with its golden tints, rules the slopes. In the woods there are anemones, bluebells, wood sorrel, foxgloves and primroses, but these disappear as one climbs higher.

The lower slopes of the fells are also home to many animals, particularly the red deer, fox and red squirrel, a species not yet driven out by the grey squirrel as in other parts of England. Even at high altitude there are colonies of voles providing food for the

predatory birds that live among the crags of the summits. The raven is the most prolific of the birds of the upper fells and with their skilful aerobatics as they ride the upward currents of air they provide a memorable spectacle for climbers; at these altitudes there are also falcons and, though it has only recently returned to the Lake District after an absence of nearly two hundred years, the golden eagle, its state still being somewhat precarious.

Conservation and detailed study of the flora and fauna of the Lake District is still at an early stage and much work is being done in this respect for the pleasure of those who will visit England's largest National Park. Much work is also essential to keep the very fabric of the region in good heart, and nowhere is this more important than in the central fells area.

The great central massif from which the major lakes of the Lake District radiate is the wildest and least 'touristy' part of the Lake

District, with just a few roads penetrating into the valleys leading up to the fells, where there are no roads. To enjoy the high fells, therefore, it is essential to walk. This is no exploratory ordeal, for over the centuries many feet have trodden out paths over passes, across fells and up to summits, in some cases in such numbers that what was originally a narrow path has become a walkers' highway.

This has led to some anxiety among conservationists and those who appreciate that English Lakeland is an unique and irreplaceable part of the British countryside. Unless numbers of visitors are limited, conservationists believe, it is inevitable that the wear and tear on Britain's most glorious mountains and lakes caused by the thousands of boots which trudge over and around them will continue. Fortunately, the dangers have been foreseen by the Lake District's governing and planning authorities and a constant battle against decay and destruction is waged by such bodies as the National Park authorities, the National Trust and the Forestry Commission as well as by members of the public who are keenly aware of the value of this piece of national heritage.

Inevitably, the great central fells, the greatest challenge motivating walkers in the Lake District, are most at risk, for the numbers who come to climb them increases every year. This is partly because the area of the central fells is small and its boundaries are well defined by the valleys which provide a way into them. To the south, these include the Langdale and Duddon valleys; and there is the Hardknott Pass and Eskdale, the valley of which begins in the fells themselves between Bow Fell and the Scafell Pikes. The western boundary of the high fells is marked by Wast Water and Wasdale, a popular route for a direct assault on the Scafells.

Although many keen walkers start their climbs into the central fells from well-equipped centres like Ambleside or smaller points like Elterwater, increasing numbers of people tend to make full use of the many car parks provided by the local authorities and drive as near as possible to the start of their chosen climb. One of the most popular, and the prettiest, motorists' routes into the central fells area is from Borrowdale, which also is the start of the Honister Pass, from the top of which there are other routes that save at least 1000 feet (305 metres) of walking and climbing.

Many people using the lovely Borrowdale approach start their walk into the central fells at Rosthwaite, climbing either via

Coombe Gill, a glacial hanging valley and up to Glaramara, the summit with a charming name and glorious views, or they approach via Stonethwaite Beck and Langstrath Beck, a long valley with a path off to Stake Pass. At the summit of 2560-foot (780-metre) Glaramara the remains of a Stone Age axe factory have been found, while the name of the mountain, which means 'shepherd's hut', suggests that it has been a recognized meeting point over centuries.

To the west, Ennerdale, down which the River Liza flows into Ennerdale Water, offers car-parking places near Ennerdale village and the western end of the lake, and many paths, most of them steep, up to Red Pike and along to High Stile, High Crag and beyond, while a popular way up to Great Gable is from the head of the valley. Most walkers consider, however, that the best way up to Red Pike and High Stile is from Buttermere (itself well-served by roads), taking in Sour Milk Gill and Bleaberry Tarn on the way, while the demanding slopes of Great Gable can also be reached from Wasdale Head and from Seathwaite in Borrowdale.

For walkers approaching from the east, the Langdale Valley, as lovely in its way as

OPPOSITE, TOP LEFT
Rock-climbing is a popular Lake District activity and numerous activity and sports centres cater for people at all levels of experience .

OPPOSITE, TOP RIGHT
The splendid outline of the Langdale Pikes dominates the head of Great Langdale, photographed from near Loughrigg Tarn .

OPPOSITE, BELOW
A bright clear day, and the Honister Pass, which links Borrowdale and Buttermere, looks less formidable than usual. The pass has a one-in-four gradient on its west side and on a grey day its scree-scarred slopes can look quite alarming. From the top of the pass, which is at 1176 feet (358.5 metres) above sea level, there is a good route for walkers to Great Gable.

ABOVE
The descent from the high fells into Borrowdale, by Styhead Gill, which flows down from Styhead Tarn between Great Gable and Seathwaite Fell .

RIGHT
High Stile, with Buttermere beyond, seen from Windy Gap, between Great Gable and Green Gable .

OVERLEAF
Wasdale and Wast Water, photographed from the summit of Great Gable. The cairn in the foreground is the Westmorland Cairn, one of two cairns on the mountain.

Borrowdale, gives access by car to the foot of the Langdale Pikes and to Bow Fell. From near the New Dungeon Ghyll hotel, once a farm, the Langdale Pikes can be seen looming above the valley, their various crags making an impressive horizon. The well-worn path climbing alongside Stickle Gill reaches to Stickle Tarn, which was artificially enlarged in the 19th century as a reservoir for gunpowder works at Elterwater. From here, Pavey Ark, Harrison Stickle and Loft Crag can be readily identified and, though the gradient is steep, the actual distance as the crow flies between valley floor and the Langdale Pikes is not more than a mile.

To the west of the Langdale Pikes is 2960-foot (902-metre) Bow Fell, which can be approached either from the Borrowdale side or from Langdale. This latter, southern approach begins at the point where the B6848 turns south to the valley of the Brathay river. The climb begins over the spur of hill known as The Bond which lies between the Mickleden valley and Oxendale. This starts off as an easy walk over a grass-covered slope which becomes more rocky as one gains height and there are rewarding views of the Langdale Valley looking back and Bow Fell ahead. An alternative route is via Pike O'Blisco and then on via Crinkle Crags to the Three Tarns, near which the path is joined by

the more used route over The Bond. The rest of the walk to the summit is undemanding and provides a view that explains its popularity; Scafell Pike, Crinkle Crags, Langdale Pikes and the valleys of Eskdale, Langdale and Langstrath are all part of the panorama, with harsh rocks in the foreground and green valleys below.

Once on Bow Fell, walkers are tempted to go on to Crinkle Crags, for the two summits are joined by a ridge. Crinkle Crags gets its name from its corrugated appearance, the result of the broken terrain which is full of gullies and cracks and strewn with boulders which do not make easy walking.

Many of the paths in this area of the central fells seem to lead inevitably to Angle Tarn and Esk Haus, especially the latter, which is a great meeting of the ways and in summer can look as busy as a walkers' Piccadilly Circus. Here, most walkers, if they are on the way up, will be heading for Scafell and Scafell Pike, the high points, in every sense of the word, of the central fells.

Once on Scafell, some climbers feel a sense of disappointment for the summit lacks drama, perhaps because of its well-used look and -almost inevitably - the presence of other walkers. The flat top is strewn with boulders and the summit cairn, which once gave a

focus of interest, is in ruins as a result of its popularity among the thousands who have climbed over it. On a fine day, however, the view more than compensates for any disappointment.

An alternative and less crowded route to Scafell and Scafell Pike is from Wasdale, a starting point that deters many who do not want the long drive round to the west and the way to Wast Water. It is worth the extra effort, however, not only for the sheer beauty of the lake itself but because the climb from Wasdale Head to Brown Tongue and then up to Scafell is relatively easy and offers good views of the Scafell crags.

From here, everyone who has achieved the feat of arriving at the top of England feels an uplifting of the spirit which higher mountains and more magnificent views cannot equal. Lakeland's fells make a personal appeal to every visitor, of a kind which William Wordsworth knew when he wrote in 'The Rainbow':

> *'My heart leaps up when I behold*
> *A rainbow in the sky:*
> *So it was when my life began;*
> *So it is now I am a man;*
> *So be it when I shall grow old,*
> *Or let me die!'*